A SCOT AT WESTMINSTER

A SCOT AT WESTMINSTER

DONALD STEWART

Edited with new material by
Mary Stewart MacKinnon

THE
CATALONE
PRESS

Canadian Cataloguing in Publication Data
Stewart, Donald, 1920-1992
A Scot at Westminster
ISBN 0-9698337-1-7
1. Stewart, Donald 1920-1992 2. Scottish National Party -- Biography. 3. Politicians -- Great Britain -- Biography. 4. Great Britain -- Politics and government -- 1964-1979. 5. Great Britain --Politics and government -- 1979- I. MacKinnon, Mary Stewart. II. Title.

DA822.S73A3 1994   941.1085'092 C94-950142-5

Cover Photo: Angus Smith Photographic
Cover Design: Harve Grant
Printed by City Printers Ltd.,
Sydney, Nova Scotia.

Published by The Catalone Press
P.O. Box 1878
Sydney, Nova Scotia
Canada

CONTENTS

FOREWORD

When Donald Stewart, Privy Councillor and Member of Parliament for the Western Isles, retired in 1987, many friends and former colleagues suggested that he should write his memoirs. Knowing how his conversation was always seasoned with interesting and humorous anecdotes, many of which were culled from his keen observation of human nature, they felt that his recollections of seventeen years in the House of Commons, combined with his easy journalistic style, could not fail to make enjoyable reading.

At first, however, he was reluctant. In his notes he wrote, "The word 'memoirs' put me off. It sounded pretentious, implying an inflated idea of my own importance and impact on affairs." Being essentially a modest man, he was afraid that his comments on abler and better men would appear patronising. Eventually he came round to the idea that as a Scottish Nationalist from the Western Isles he had a unique standpoint and that his reactions and attitude to the House of Commons might be of interest, as well as his views on politicians whose names are well-known.

Unfortunately, before he had quite completed the book, he suffered a heart attack and died in August, 1992. I was familiar with his writing, for he had on several occasions given me chapters to read, and I offered to do the final editing and prepare the manuscript for publication. He had hoped to add two or three more chapters, but even without them, his writing is packed with fascinating material, representing many facets of parliamentary life during his incumbency as Member of Parliament for the Western isles. I am most grateful to Chrissie, his widow, who stood at his side for 37 years and who was a real helpmeet to him in all his endeavours, for giving me access to his manuscript and all his notes and also for her assistance and input in the chapter on the S.N.P. It was a privilege for me to undertake this one last task on behalf of Donald, who was always my well-loved big brother.

Mary Stewart MacKinnon.
Arnish, Cape Breton, Nova Scotia.
May, 1994.

1: EARLY DAYS

Friday, 19 June, 1970. The British electorate had voted in the General Election the previous day, but due to the geographical spread of the inhabited islands of the Western Isles, it was necessary to collect the ballot boxes by fishery cruiser, and hence the result was almost 24 hours behind the rest of Britain. (In recent elections the boxes have been collected by helicopter which has enabled the Western Isles result to be announced among the first few.)

The islands' branches and the activists of the Scottish National Party had campaigned in a strong challenge to Labour, and we were confident of a good showing, although only the most optimistic entertained the possibility that we could beat Malcolm MacMillan who had held the seat for the Labour Party since 1935.

As the counting and checking went on in the Drill Hall at Stornoway it became clear that we were at least running level with Labour, but it was not until the Police Superintendent, John MacLeod, whispered to me, "Prepare your speech as head of the poll," that I really came to terms with the likelihood that I was to be the new Member of Parliament.

When the Sheriff announced the result the majority was slender, but it was enough:

Donald Stewart (SNP)	6568
M.K. MacMillan (Labour)	5842
R.M. MacLeod (Conservative)	2822
Majority	726

As the *Scotsman* said, it was "an incredible last-gap breakthrough by the SNP, "particularly as Winnie Ewing had lost her seat at Hamilton which she had taken from Labour in a sensational overturn of a 16,000 majority in 1967, and it looked as if the brief but productive presence of the SNP at Westminster was over for another long hiatus. Our result was the first time that the Party had won a seat at a General Election and it ended the taunts that the SNP could make a showing at by-elections but that faced with forming a government, the public would revert to the established parties.

I had promised earlier in the day to pass on the result to Winnie Ewing, and when Chrissie and I had managed to detach ourselves from the crowd offering congratulations and good wishes, we were driven home and I phoned Winnie at her house in Glasgow. A number of leading members of the Party had gathered there, in a depressed mood after the Party's defeats in all other seats. The call was answered by the Party Chairman, Billy Wolfe, and when I told him, "I'm in," I could hear the room erupt in hysterical delight. Later that evening at our victory celebration at the Crown Inn in Stornoway, I was called to the telephone repeatedly to take calls from all over Scotland and beyond. It was clear that our win had revived the Party's spirits and hopes.

Before moving off to Westminster, let me provide a few biographical details to set the scene...

I was born in the town of Stornoway in 1920. At the time, although I do not recall it, the house was one of several in the town with a roof of thatch. There was still one thatched house within the burgh at the start of the Second World War.

Stornoway was a grand place for boys to grow up in. There was no end to the diversions and ploys we could and did invent. We fished for cuddies and mackerel and sometimes more exotic fish, around the piers and wharves; we jumped in and out of boats of which there were hundreds in the fishing season, drifters from Buckie, Peterhead, Yarmouth and Lowestoft, as well as the local fleet. The herring industry was the mainstay of employment in the town in the 1920s, as acknowledged in the motto on the town coat of arms: *God's Providence is Our Inheritance.* We had the run of the hundreds of acres of the grounds of Lews Castle and beyond that, the wide open moors of the island, with numberless lochs providing free fishing for brown trout.

The local school was the Nicolson Institute. It had, and still has, an excellent scholastic record, with a high percentage of its pupils going on to university and excelling in different professions in Scotland and throughout the world. In my day, most of the teachers were authoritarian in the predominant teaching fashion of the time, although there were a few on whom I look back with respect and affection.

I left school at the age of 16 to take a job as a junior clerk in a local solicitor's office. I was aware that my parents could not afford to send me to university, even if my marks had been better than they were, and I felt I should be earning as soon as possible. In my last two years at school I was simply marking time until a suitable job turned up. Looking back, I would rather have had a university education than not, but – as the Gaelic expresses it – "it wasn't put out for me" so I have never wasted any time bemoaning the lack of it.

After three years in the solicitor's office, I was offered and accepted a position on the office staff of Kenneth MacKenzie Limited, a leading manufacturer of Harris Tweed, employing over 200 in their mills and with about 700 self-employed weavers on their books. Two years later, with the Second World War in progress, I was called up to the Royal Navy. Having been a member of the Stornoway Sea Cadet Corps for seven years and fairly proficient in Morse and semaphore signalling, I opted for the signals branch. I spent five years in the war-time navy. On demob I rejoined my old firm where I remained for 25 years until my election to Parliament; by that time I had become a director of the company.

In 1951 I accepted an invitation from some local people to allow my name to be entered in the coming election to Stornoway Town Council. In this contest I came in second of the three successful candidates from a field of five. I served as a Councillor for almost 20 years, filling the offices of Dean of Guild, Junior Bailie and Senior Bailie successively, until elected Provost in 1959. At the end of my three-year term I was again elected as Provost and served until 1965, when I declined nomination. I was elected again to that office in 1968 and was still serving when I was elected to Parliament. From my time as a Bailie I also served as a magistrate in the Burgh Police Court and was sworn in by the Sheriff-Principal as an Honorary Sheriff in 1960 and, although excused from this duty during my time at Westminster, since my retirement I still occasionally get called to take a Court.

As it turned out, I went to the House of Commons fairly conversant with the main concerns of my constituency. One of the bodies on which I served in my local government years was the Stornoway Trust Estate which, through the generosity of the first Lord Leverhulme, belonged to the local people. The estate comprised the Burgh of Stornoway and an area which extended about twenty miles around the town, including over a score of crofting villages. The fishing industry I knew from my early days; Harris Tweed (by 1970 the main industry of Lewis) I knew from 30 years' employment; and, having served 20 years in local government, I was aware of the constraints on local government finance, procedures of meetings, the relationship between local and central government, etc. So, fortuitously, from this background I was armed in some part to do battle on behalf of my electorate, and although realizing that I was entering new terrain, I felt that I would not be entirely defenceless on some vital issues.

2: POLITICAL EDUCATION

In my school days a fire was lit in my imagination by the struggle of Wallace and Bruce to maintain the independence of Scotland, but my total conversion to the case for an independent Scotland took place during the General Election in 1935 when Sir Alexander MacEwen fought the Western Isles in the Nationalist cause. The staking of the nation's claim advanced by this tall, eagle-visaged figure convinced me that here was a goal worthy of the support and dedication of the Scottish people in a national movement to recover our lost freedom and to move to an exciting future, taking our rightful place in the family of free nations.

I wrote to SNP Headquarters in Glasgow in 1936, expressing my wish to join the ranks and asking for details of the Party's aims and policies. An indication of how thin on the ground Nationalists were at that time could be judged by the reply which offered to put me in touch with a Party member in Inverness, a Mr. MacNeill. Years later I got to know D.H. MacNeill, an Inverness solicitor, author of *The Scottish Constitution* and a stalwart Nationalist.

In those days to meet another Nationalist was almost as unusual as the Livingstone/Stanley encounter in Africa. The public perception of Scottish Nationalists was of a minority of kilted cranks whose odd notions would never win the acceptance of the Scottish people. It was similar to the current attitude to the Green Party, whose policies will be winning substantial support in a few years time.

14

In passing, I may mention Douglas Hurd's speeches in Scotland in the '92 election, when he said he would be saddened if he had to visit Scotland 'as a foreign country'. Curiously enough, one of the few 'Nats' I knew forty years ago was his uncle, Robert Hurd, who, as a town planner and an architect, was retained by Stornoway Town Council. He was a member of the National Executive of the SNP.

The earliest evidence of membership of the Party which I can trace is a card signed by Arthur Donaldson dated 1944, while I was still serving in the Navy. From the mid 1930s, however, concurrently with holding Nationalist views, I became a convert to the organization of society on the basis of Socialism, so that Nationalist and Socialist views ran in tandem. Needless to say, I was a regular reader of *The Scots Independent* but also became a regular reader of Tom Johnston's *Forward* and the ILP's *New Leader*. The process was helped on by books such as *The Ragged-trousered Philanthropists,* Jack London's *The Iron Heel,* Bernard Shaw's *The Intelligent Woman's Guide to Socialism,* and membership of the Left Book Club. The launching by Gollanz of the Left Book Club was a tremendous boost for Left-wing ideas. Once a month, at a cost of half-a-crown, a book of lively, topical and exciting contents, written always from a Left perspective, landed on thousands of doorsteps. From hindsight it is clear that the LBC platform was confined to the Stalinist interpretation and that conflicting ideas – for example, Trotsky's – would hardly ever get a look-in.

Prior to the Second World War, the policies of the Labour Party included Home Rule for Scotland. I thought I could achieve two ends in one – a Socialist Scotland – by joining the Labour party, which I did in 1937. Some years later that redoubtable fighter for Scotland, Oliver Brown, told me that he had taken the same step with the same objective in mind.

I drifted out of the Labour Party in 1939, having in the interval become disillusioned, like most of the younger members, by the apparent lack of conviction in the leadership, which was compounded by the reactionary dead weight of the TUC bosses. In the intervening period my allegiance was switching to the ILP which seemed to me composed of Socialists who took seriously the ideals of a Socialist society and intended the abolition of the capitalist system. As the ILP was under attack by the Communist Party for association with Trotskyist groups, the anti-Stalinist aspect was prominent, and for that reason I never had any illusions about Stalin and his regime, when people who should have known or did know better were pimping for Stalin, testifying to the genuineness of the Moscow Trials and generally boosting the Soviet Union as a worker's paradise. Despite this, I never accepted the Cold War propaganda that unless we were armed to the teeth – nuclear weapons and all – the Russians were poised to invade the West.

During my service in the Navy, I developed my interest in the Nationalist cause, regularly renewing Party membership, subscribing to the Party paper, and buying pamphlets produced by the SNP and other Nationalist organizations. When the ships in which I served lay at anchor at Greenock, I would travel to Glasgow to listen to Oliver Brown speaking at open-air stances. Oliver was unique as a propagandist, with a blend of fact, comment and wit that gripped the listener. He made a massive contribution to the cause of Scotland.

Douglas Young, a university lecturer from Tayside, had been elected Chairman of the Scottish National Party in 1942 by members who were dissatisfied with John McCormick's leadership. He refused to comply with the British Government's military conscription of the Scots and was sentenced to a year's imprisonment. His appeal was dismissed and he served his sentence less the usual remission. In February 1944, Douglas Young was the SNP candidate in a by-election in Kirkcaldy Burghs. Under the war-time truce between the parties, the Tories did not contest, and the Labour candidate, a Mr. T.F. Hubbard, received 8,268 votes. Despite widespread misunderstanding and misrepresentation of his stand, Young caused a sensation by securing 6,621 votes. A month after the by-election he was charged, at the instigation of the Ministry presided over by the Labour Minister Ernest Bevin, with non-compliance with British industrial conscription and was sentenced to a further term of imprisonment.

Young appeared to me as the leader Scotland had waited for over a long period. His espousal of the Scottish cause and his courageous moral stand in a war-time climate, lifted him to the heroic level in my eyes. I felt a sense of betrayal when, in the late 1940s, he resigned from the SNP and defected to the Labour Party. But by the end of the first post-war Labour government, Douglas Young had lost his illusions of the Labour Party and published a pamphlet entitled *Labour Record of Scotland: Unfulfilled Pledges Exposed.* As Mrs. Naomi Mitchison said in her foreword:

> This pamphlet is by a socialist who is deeply disturbed, as I am too, by the fact that the Labour Government made certain promises about Scotland before it came to power, has not so far kept them and does not appear to be going to do so.

They were neither the first nor the last Socialists who had to face this fact.

A by-election took place in Motherwell in April 1945. The SNP candidate was Dr. Robert McIntyre. During the campaign I had gone down to Motherwell to see how the fight was going but saw little sign in the town in the couple of hours I spent there of public interest in the election. On the day the result was announced I was serving on H.M.S. *Celandine,* a Flower class corvette, and was listening, in the middle of the Atlantic, to a late evening broadcast from the BBC. The bulletin was mainly taken up with the news of the death of President Roosevelt, but towards the end the announcer, in the round-up of miscellaneous items, said that a party known as the Scottish National Party had won a by-election in Motherwell. I can still recall my feelings.

Here at last was the dawn of a new day for our country. The nation was poised for independence once the war ended. Alas, it was to take another twenty years before a similar victory was achieved.

3: THE HOUSE IN 1970

Several well-known names became casualties in the General Election of 1970. These included George Brown, Jennie Lee (Aneurin Bevan's widow), Robert Maxwell, Professor Esmond Wright, Woodrow Wyatt and Donald Dewar. Only the last came back to the Commons.

Apart from myself, among new arrivals that year were Neil Kinnock, Winston Churchill, Dennis Skinner, Rev. Ian Paisley, John Smith, Norman Tebbit and Gerald Kaufman.

Looking back, it seems to me that the House contained far more 'characters' then than in later years. This applies all round, but is particularly conspicuous on the Tory side, where the new recruits in the '80s appear to have been produced from an identical mould, having as much individuality as a sheet of postage stamps.

Most of the old characters are gone, through death or retirement, but will be remembered by those who knew them and enjoyed their contribution to the House of Commons and often to the gaiety of the nation. A Tory, David James, sat for a Dorset seat but was also domiciled in a castle in Mull. David, ex RNVR, had taken part in two Antarctic expeditions, but his fame arose from his escape from a prison camp in Germany in World War II. On the run he wore his naval uniform, and passed himself off as an officer of the Bulgarian Navy, calculating that the Germans would be no better acquainted with that navy than everyone else. He had forged documents and in order to present a name which could be kept in mind, these were in the name of "I. Bagerov". He must have had great satisfaction, when challenged, in giving his name.

Bob Edwards (Labour) had led an ILP contingent from Britain to the Republican side in the Spanish Civil War. Physically a little man, he would squash a proposition from the extreme Left by putting his head back, looking down his nose and saying, "That's not what Trotsky said to me."

Gerald Nabarro (Tory) was a familiar name and an even more familiar face to the British public at that time. An ex-sergeant major who had risen in the world, his fruity voice, handlebar moustache (which he would comb on TV) and his idiosyncratic opinions were immediately recognizable. A good deal of the time he acted a part, but he was a formidable debater, being well-informed on subjects like coal and steel, and he ran a successful campaign against some of the dottier aspects of purchase tax.

John Robertson (Labour) was a man whose abilities should have carried him much further than they did. Few in his party had such an extensive knowledge of Socialist philosophy and history and practical experience of Trade Union leadership. Always a robust defender of Scottish interests, he broke with Labour to join Jim Sillars in founding the Scottish Labour Party. It was highly enlightening to listen to John's prognosis of political developments.

Neil Marten (Tory) was one of these independent minds that are respected across the political spectrum. I got to know him well through mutual opposition to membership of the Common Market. In the early '70s, as chairman of the British-Norwegian Group, he led a party of MPs, of which I was a member, on a trip to Norway. When Neil retired I was honoured to be elected in his place as Chairman of the Group.

Simon Mahon (Labour) sat for a Liverpool seat. He was a tall man with an erect military bearing. He was an excellent speaker, although he rarely took part in debates, and he was very helpful to new members. He sticks in my mind because of a story he told me about a visit to a house in his constituency. A large hairy dog was lying across the step and as the lady of the house opened the door the animal bounded inside. The hound then snatched a cake from a tea-tray put out for Simon, and the hostess ignored it. Later it walked over to a table and, cocking its leg, left a puddle on the floor. Simon wondered to himself why they didn't train their pet but decided it was none of his business. Going down the path when his visit was concluded, he was considerably put out by a shout from the lady of the house: "Mr. Mahon, aren't you taking your dog with you?"

Sir Fitzroy Maclean (Tory) was a diplomat and soldier and wartime chum of Marshal Tito. Although amusing in private conversation, his speeches in the House would not put the heather on fire and were delivered in a dull monotone. I used to ask myself, is this the man who wrote these scintillating books?

Willie Hamilton (Labour) was always very much in action, usually harrying the Royal Family, mainly on the grounds of their expensive hangers-on. He was absolutely fearless in expressing his views, saying aloud what others would say behind their hands. He represented a seat in Fife and it was curious the number of people who took him for a Scot although he hails from the North of England. He was regarded as an extreme Left-winger, probably because of his Royals-bashing but was in fact on the Right wing of the Labour Party.

Sir Hugh Fraser (Tory) was another of the 'man o' independent mind' tendency. Before my time, Hugh had filled government office but was a back-bencher when I knew him. He was active in that role and there were few big occasions without a trenchant and amusing sally from him. A brother of Lord Lovat, he kept up an interest in developments in the Highlands. At the request of the Speaker, I represented him at Hugh's funeral near Beauly. It was a bright but cold day, and after the service in the chapel and the interment, girls with trays bearing glasses of malt whisky went round the churchyard – a civilised touch of which Hugh would have approved.

Gerry Fitt (now Lord Fitt) must be one of the most courageous men of the times. He could be under fire from both sides of the Northern Ireland divide but consistently attacked injustices to his own community while maintaining the fight against men of violence. He had some unpleasant experiences at his home in Belfast, including an invasion by armed men which he repelled, and a silent vigil opposite his house with a large mob holding torches aloft.

He moved house to London and once while telephoning Lady Fitt from a House of Lords corridor, his little grand-daughter took the phone saying, "Baa baa black sheep," the start of the nursery rhyme which Gerry had been teaching her. So Gerry was reciting the rhyme over the phone when he became aware of somebody standing behind him, and turning round he saw Lord Denning listening with interest to his colleague slowly enunciating "Have you any wool?" The old judge quickly sized up the situation saying,

"Ah, no doubt you are making a statement to the Irish Press."

As well as these outstanding Members, there were knights of the shires, a few Brigadiers, an Admiral, and, it seems to me, a more mixed bag of odd-balls around in the early '70s. There were unique characters in the House throughout my time there, and I will recall some of them at a later stage.

4: THE CENOTAPH ISSUE

The theory that the Westminster Parliament is in fact the English Parliament continuing was reinforced by the actions of the Home Office in the matter of representation at the Cenotaph. It was the wish of the SNP Group that I, as Party Leader, should be allowed to attend the Remembrance Service at the Cenotaph and lay a wreath with the other parties. Our Whip applied each year on my behalf and each time was turned down by successive Home Secretaries, Roy Jenkins and Merlyn Rees for Labour, and Leon Brittan for the Tories.

The attitude of the Home Office gave rise to resentment and anger in places and individuals in Scotland not normally supportive of the SNP. Letters critical of the Home Office appeared in the Press, John Junor attacked the decision in his column in the *Sunday Express,* and the *Daily Record* did likewise in an editorial. As the *Record* pointed out, on the first occasion I was the only Party leader among Harold Wilson, Margaret Thatcher and Jeremy Thorpe, entitled to stand at the Cenotaph wearing wartime service medals.

On behalf of the SNP Group, Douglas Henderson wrote in June 1975 to the Home Secretary, Roy Jenkins, about the Cenotaph ceremony to be held in November and received the following reply:

> Home Office, Whitehall, London.
>
> I of course understand the Scottish Nationalist Party's wish to be associated with this national act of remembrance, and I have, as I did last year, given

your request careful thought. I am afraid, however, that I am not persuaded that it would be appropriate at this juncture, to make changes in the form of ceremony by extending official representation to include leaders of political parties other than those operating on a United Kingdom basis; since at this central ceremony at Westminster (as distinct from those held elsewhere in the country) it is on behalf of the United Kingdom as a whole that the Government and the political parties have been regarded as participating.

There was an amusing sequel to this in 1983 when Dr. David Owen, in his speech to the Annual Conference of the Social-Democratic Party, complained of the petty spite of the Government in refusing to allow the Leader of the SDP to take part in the Armistice Ceremony at the Cenotaph. The then Leader of the SDP was Roy Jenkins.

When Leon Brittan as Home Secretary of the Tory Government changed the formula in 1984, he dropped the 'explanation' offered by Jenkins to Douglas Henderson and produced a new exclusion clause. The new criterion was:

The leaders of Parties having at least six seats in the House of Commons following the last General Election will be invited to attend the Ceremony and to lay a wreath while Leaders of Parties with more than one but less than six seats following the Election will be invited to attend but not to lay wreaths.

Now reduced to two Members, the SNP was cut out from wreath-laying but it allowed David Owen's party of seven to take part in what had been refused to the SNP with eleven. The Brits have had long experience of moving the goalposts.

5: OTHER ISSUES IN THE HOUSE

Apart from the day-to-day watch on Scottish issues which I pursued as far as possible, and the subsequent sniping at Question Time to air or further them, I took my part in a number of on-going campaigns.

One of the most sustained over my Parliamentary time involved supporting attempts to amend the Abortion Act of 1967 which was pushed through by David Steel with the help of Roy Jenkins. The destruction of life arising from this Act, although euphemistically spoken of as a matter of 'termination of pregnancy', has been abhorrent to me.

While accepting that there are circumstances which render an abortion unavoidable, the effect of the Act in practice became virtually abortion on demand. In passing, I should remark on the numerous occasions where assurances were given to quieten doubters, and how they fell by the board with the passage of time. Accordingly, each time that a Member submitted a Bill to reduce the effects of the Act – usually in the permitted time-scale – I felt obliged to speak and vote in support of the amendment.

The opposition to these Private Member's Bills on this issue was sustained and horrendous. In each case the Member concerned was the recipient of appalling abuse, vile communications, and threats of deselection. They had to run the gauntlet of attacks, often personal, during debates in the House, although of course, the observations made then were on a more circumspect level than in private correspondence.

Those of us who were backing amending legislation spent a number of Fridays in London in order to take part. In one of these debates I quoted from an article by Mr. Malcolm Muggeridge in the *Sunday Times* of the previous week. A day or two later I received a letter from Mr. Muggeridge:

> Dear Mr. Stewart,
> I should like to thank you for quoting from my article on abortion in your House of Commons speech. It gave me great satisfaction, especially as you chose precisely the words I should have wished might be repeated. It was the more pleasing because the Sunday Times subs – I am sure pro-abortionists to a man – had done their best to bury the article out of sight among the letters to the editor.
>
> Yours sincerely,
> Malcolm Muggeridge

In spite of these efforts nothing has been done to alter the Abortion Act substantially, and I will deal with the difficulties met by Private Members' Bills at a later stage.

*   *   *

Although I would not claim that I had anything like the total dedication to the cause of the disabled shown by Members like Jack Ashley, John Hannam and Alf Morris, it was an issue to which I was always ready to give my support. I became active on behalf of 'Disablement Income Group Scotland' whose aim was 'to secure the financial rights and general welfare of disabled people'.

By the luck of the draw, I came fairly high on the list of Members entitled to introduce a Private Bill of their own choosing to the House, and following an approach from Jack Ashley, I presented a Bill to make life easier in various respects for disabled people. I will tell later of the fate of my bill.

*   *   *

While I have always regarded Anti-Semitism as an irrational and abhorrent prejudice, I developed a strongly critical attitude towards the actions of the state of Israel with regard to the Palestinians. Taking a lead from the backing of the United States for Israel, the rest of the world has gone along with the flouting of United Nations resolutions by the Israelis.

There are voices of sanity raised in Israel urging justice for the Palestinian people, but unfortunately in recent years the hard-liners like Begin, Shamir and Sharon have had all the running. The legitimacy of the Palestinian claim has been reinforced by the rush of Israeli settlements on the West Bank.

Israel appears to be impervious to denunciation of her actions, describing critics as 'simply anti-Semites'. The United Nations should not allow this propaganda to affect their concern for a just settlement of the problem, nor be taken in by references to disputed lands as 'Samaria and Judea'.

The history of the Highland Clearances gave me an affinity with the plight of the Palestinians and gave rise to my interventions in the Commons on the matter. Since Israel is a client state of the United States, the responsibility of America to press for a solution cannot be avoided and the urgency is underlined by the influx of Jews from the Soviet Union adding to the pressure on the land.

6: THE 'POWER' OF MPs

It is a cherished illusion of the Brits that their system of government at Westminster is the envy of the world. They assert the proposition as a fact often enough. Mrs. Thatcher rattled on about the Prime Minister being 'directly answerable to Parliament' but this exists only when it suits. Take, for example, the period when serious questions were being asked about the integrity of her Cabinet Secretary and Attorney-General during the 'Spycatcher' affair – she managed to evade explanations for long enough.

There is an old story about two MPs who lost their way while motoring and ended up in a ploughed field. After some time a farmer appeared on the scene and was asked if he could tell the stranded motorists where they were.

"Yur in this 'ere meadow," he said, at which one of the Members remarked to his companion that the response was a perfect Parliamentary answer: "It's short, it's true, and it tells you damn all you didn't know before."

This comment is accurate enough concerning most of the replies to Parliamentary Questions. The Table Office in the House of Commons where questions are lodged by Members has a list of subjects which are unacceptable for appearing on the Order Paper. True, many of these are reasonable, such as references to organizations for which there is no ministerial responsibility. It is when the Minister and his Civil Service aides put their heads together to dilute the release of information that Members are frustrated.

Even when an answer is provided which seems to satisfy the demands of the Question, it frequently turns out to be negative information. Take, for example, this exchange from November 30, 1983:

Question: How often does the Radiochemical Inspectorate inspect sites licensed for the disposal of radioactive wastes?

Answer: The number of visits is determined by the radiological significance of the disposal.

It is obvious from this 'reply' that the Member who put the Question will be neither wiser nor better informed.

Another escape route for Ministries reluctant to provide details on which Members may attack the government is the formula, which appears from time to time in Parliamentary Answers, that "the expenditure necessary to supply this information would not be justified". Even in the vaunted Parliamentary watchdogs, the Select Committees, Ministers and Civil Servants are showing a growing reluctance to give specific answers, and there is the outright refusal to answer such as Nicholas Ridley showed in an investigation while he was head of the Department of Trade.

In recent times the power of decision-making by backbench Members has been steadily eroded. Nowadays power rests with the Cabinet (a process accelerated under Margaret Thatcher), multinational companies, Whitehall, and increasingly, the EEC Commission. A Member's contribution to the process of law-making is minute, if not non-existent. Even amendments to legislation (unless government sponsored) are rarely accepted.

Seldom, too, is the vote at the end of a Debate influenced by the arguments put forward in speeches; too many

Members are simply lobby fodder, submitting to their Whips to point them in the direction of the correct lobby. The number of Party hacks is depressingly high. On February 14, 1980, a debate took place on the fishing industry in which Tory MPs, among others, demanded urgent financial aid for the industry. A fortnight later there was a vote on a Government proposal to increase the levy on fish landings by £1$^1/_2$ million, a substantial extra burden to carry at a time of difficulty. The proposal was supported by 13 Tory MPs from Scotland, including some who had been vociferous in demanding aid two weeks previously! The Labour Party, too, has its own quota, always available to be rounded up and coralled by the cowboys of their Whips' Office.

Then there is the 'payroll' vote – an assured support column of 100 or more Ministers and Under-Secretaries, down to PPSs in Government jobs who will invariably back the Government's wishes. Perhaps even more loyal than these are the back-benchers panting for promotion in a future re-shuffle of posts.

The power of Members, such as it is, consists in using the House as a sounding board in the hope that their ideas, by being taken up by the Press, will fall on fruitful ground among the general public. MP's have some muscle in voting if the vote is close; but principally their effectiveness lies in finding solutions to the problems of their constituents. The reader may be asking, "But what about Private Members' Bills?" I will deal with this in the next chapter.

7: MY PRIVATE MEMBER'S BILLS

On the face of it, the opportunity for Members to introduce Bills of their own choosing seems a powerful weapon for advancing causes near to their heart. However, the obstacles against a backbench Member getting a Bill through are formidable, and it is extremely rare for Bills making major changes to reach the Statute Book. David Steel's Abortion Act was one of the exceptions, but it would cost nothing to the Exchequer and it was aided by support from the Labour Home Secretary, Roy Jenkins.

The first hurdle is that one enters a ballot for 20 places out of over 600 MPs, although not all bother to try. In my 17 years in the House I was successful on three occasions, which is well above average. The second hazard is that the debate on such Bills is confined to Fridays and only a handful of such slots are allocated as the Government will have booked half for their own business. A further obstacle is that opponents of your Bill can 'talk it out' by filibustering until 2:30 p.m. when the House rises on a Friday. Other Bills on the list are read out by title only and it requires only one Member to shout 'Object!' and no further progress can be made that day. It can then be submitted on subsequent Fridays but if objection is still offered, it joins legions of lost Bills.

There is an even more fundamental constitutional issue involved in Government attitude to Private Members' Bills. On at least six occasions in my time in Parliament, Bills were introduced under the Private Members' legislation to make changes in the Abortion Act. On each occasion the Bill on Second Reading received a substantial cross-party majority vote in support. Yet none of these Bills became law because a determined minority were able, by using procedures of the House, to frustrate the will of the majority. This surely is a negation of democracy which cries out for change.

Coming 13th in the ballot for Private Members' Bills in 1978, I decided on a piece of consumer protection which I called the "Supply of Goods (Amendment) Bill". It had the backing of the Consumers' Associations both in Scotland and England and was intended to clear up the confusion about the degree of protection which had changed over a period of time from 'Would a reasonable consumer accept such goods' to the less satisfactory 'Are the goods substantially fit for their normal job'. In other words, a car, even if the engine carried you from A to B, should not be regarded as a reasonable buy if the doors kept falling off.

After a talk with a minister from the Department of Trade, the Government undertook to refer the matter to the Law Commission sitting on Consumer Protection. David Tench, Legal Officer of the Consumer Association, wrote to me expressing their pleasure at the outcome and thanking me for getting these points investigated much earlier than otherwise, but I cannot say now if it improved protection at the end of the day.

On my second lucky draw I introduced a Bill to improve the position and status of the Gaelic language. It had three aims:

      (1) To give increased choice to pupils to choose Gaelic
          as a school language;

(2) To give the language equal status to the level of Welsh in Wales;

(3) Some improvement in the time allowed for broadcasting in Gaelic.

It seemed fairly non-controversial, but to my surprise it ran into violent opposition, mainly from Tory Members, although Albert McQuarrie (Tory, Aberdeen East) was a staunch supporter. Opponents of the Bill were John Mackay (Tory, Argyle), Bill Walker (Tory, Perth and East Perthshire) Iain Sproat (Tory, Aberdeen South) and even the English Tory, Douglas Hogg, a son of Lord Hailsham.

Some of the speeches by these Tories showed ignorant prejudice against Gaelic. Bill Walker's objection seemed to be based on his claim that the Black Watch found little use for it. On the day of the debate, the Bill was late in coming up, due to filibustering to delay a Bill on compulsory wearing of seatbelts and a Bill to help the disabled which had the support of no less than 260 Members. As the 2:30 deadline approached, the closure vote was moved to end discussion and secure a vote on the Bill. This requires 100 Members in favour to be successful and as it was Friday and with only 71 Scottish Members of Parliament, most of whom were in Scotland on that day, the closure vote fell, although a number of English colleagues who were in the precincts came in to vote for closure.

There was anger in Gaelic circles at the failure of the Bill, and particularly at the volume of hostility expressed by the Members mentioned above. An Comunn Gaidhealach (The Gaelic Association) quickly issued a statement dissociating their organization from any defects in the Bill, although I had taken the entire responsibility throughout. One unexpected development was that within a few weeks, Bill Walker MP presented and spoke to a Ten-Minute Rule Bill for the assistance of Gaelic! I can only assume that he had been under some pressure for his stance on my Bill. But I was so disgusted at this turn-about that I walked out of the Chamber in front of Walker holding my nose.

For my third Bill, I took over one drafted by Jack Ashley, the Labour MP who battles consistently and strenuously on behalf of the disabled and whose efforts had already won significant advances for them. The purport of the Bill was to prohibit unjustifiable discrimination against the disabled and it had support from a number of organizations with a similar aim.

Here again was a subject, one would think, that all MPs would unite around. Not a bit of it! It met with flak, but more of the 'more in sorrow than in anger' type. One opponent was Dame Jill Knight, a Tory from Birmingham. Jack Ashley, who made a vigorous contribution to the debate, accused her of using a briefing from the Department of Health. My backers resented her intervention since she was a member of the Disablement Group in the House. Fortunately another member of the Group, the Tory M.P. John Hannam, more than compensated with an excellent supportive speech.

Alas, this Bill, too, joined the limbo of the lost. The outcome confirmed my view that only innocuous subjects, with rare exceptions on unique grounds, have any chance of survival without Government backing and allocation of time.

8: BACKING THE FISHERMEN

One group whose interests I was determined to protect, as far as lay in my power, was our fishermen. I have always regarded the occupation of fishing as one of the more honourable ways of making a living. There is no exploitation of man or beast. The work is hard, and it is a dangerous calling, since the annual figures of fatalities exceeded those in mining even when the coal industry was more extensive than it is now. Accordingly, I never missed a fishing debate and was nearly always fortunate in being called to speak.

On a number of occasions I made reference to the wide gap between the protection of and financial backing for farming compared with the fishing industry. But then, farmers have a powerful lobby in Parliament, many Tories representing agricultural communities, and quite a few being farmers themselves – at least in the sense of owning farms. It was salutary to count the number of MPs eager to take part in a debate on farming matters and compare them with the number present for a fishing debate.

Even in fishing debates some Members had less than full commitment. On February 14, 1980, a debate took place during which Tory MPs, among others, demanded urgent financial help for the industry. A fortnight later there was a vote on a Government proposal to increase the levy on landings by £1½ million, thus adding to the current problems of the fishing. It was supported by 13 Tory MPs from Scotland, including a number who had been vociferous in demanding aid two weeks previously.

As I write, the current position is that 100 per cent compensation is available to farmers for mad cow disease but none for fishermen unable to fish for eight days a month. Nor is there Government support for a decommissioning scheme for boats, although other EEC countries are operating such a scheme.

While I maintained close connection with the Stornoway fleet, consulting with leaders like my old friends Jackie Morrison and Roddy Maciver – both active and outstanding skippers themselves – I kept myself informed of the interests of the industrious groups of vessels from Scalpay, Harris and the islands of Eriskay and Barra. There has been a dramatic change in the nature of the catch since my boyhood days when Stornoway harbour in the season would be filled with steam drifters, local boats, boats from the East Coast ports and some from Yarmouth and Lowestoft, all fishing for herring. Now the local boats fish mainly for prawns, white fish and mackerel.

During the seventies, owing to shrinking stocks, a moratorium was placed on herring fishing. In the House, I pressed strongly for a dispensation for two local boats using only driftnets and whose catch therefore would consist solely of mature fish, to be allowed a small quota for local consumption. This was refused. When the ban was lifted, a German trawler took in one day from local waters a catch of herring which the two boats could not have landed in three years. In my election campaign in 1970 I had warned that EEC membership would mean the end of the existing limits and would open our waters to foreign vessels.

It was because I felt a special affinity with fishermen that I supported the claims of Iceland in the Cod War of the early 70s. It seemed the grossest theft of another's inheritance for outsiders to plunder their fishing grounds – almost the sole economic resource of the people of that island.

On May 21, 1973, the Foreign Secretary, Sir Alec Douglas-Home, made a statement in the House on the Icelandic situation, describing British trawlers fishing on the high seas being "systematically harassed by Icelandic coastguard vessels." His opposite number on the Labour Front Bench, Anthony Crosland, assured him of Labour's full support and added that the Government's decision to continue backing British trawlers fishing round Iceland had been "warmly received in all the fishing ports." Other Labour Members, with Liberals and Tories, took the same line, with the exception of Eric Heffer who pointed out that "Iceland depends on its fishing and if that is taken away these people will have nothing."

The Hansard Report continues:

> Mr. Donald Stewart: *Apart from the views ex-pressed in the House, may I ask the Rt. Hon. Gentleman whether he is aware that throughout the country, in many of the fishing ports, there is by no means total support for his policy which some honourable Members pretend or imagine there is? Is he further aware that the spectacle of Great Britain claiming oil 150 miles from our shores is not a good example to set when we are seeking to prevent Iceland from protecting its sole source of income only 50 miles from its shores? Does he appreciate that the case will eventually be won by Iceland and the sooner this gunboat diplomacy comes to an end the better?*
>
> Sir Alec Douglas-Home: *I do not know whether*

there is total support in the country for this policy but on the evidence we have heard in the House today there is quite a lot of support for our action and I would have thought that it was strong majority support. Perhaps the Hon. Gentleman will tell us how long we are expected to wait, being harassed, without any retaliation whatsoever. This is one small nation using force for political purposes, and it cannot be tolerated. We are always ready to conciliate and negotiate. I hope that we will be able to resume doing so.

The Cod War dragged on for some time but in the end the British position was recognized as indefensible and so Iceland has since enjoyed the full rights to its fishing grounds.

My concern for the industry was not confined to the West Coast fleets. I was involved also with other fishing areas in Scotland and had meetings from time to time with men like Gilbert Buchan, Sandy Baird and Willie Hay. They were doughty fighters for their men but were equally supportive of fishermen elsewhere. Their demands were always reasonable in spite of lukewarm support from successive British governments. The following correspondence which I had with Mrs Thatcher speaks for itself.

18 June 1985

HOUSE OF COMMONS
LONDON SWIA OAA

The Rt. Hon. Margaret Thatcher, M.P.,
Prime Minister,
10 Downing Street,
LONDON.

Dear Prime Minister,

You may have seen reports in the Press about the anger of leaders
of the fishing industry in Scotland over an announcement that
licences were issued for 3 English freezer trawlers in breach of
regulations and that these licences are to remain in being for the
moment.

The Minister of State at the Ministry of Agriculture and Fisheries
in a written reply, agreed that the licences had been issued "owing
to a regrettable misunderstanding in my department". The Scottish
Fishermen's Federation has demanded immediate cancellation of the
licences. The licences allow a quota of mackerel and North Sea
herring and while the industry has acknowledged that freezer trawlers
have some historical presence off the West Coast, they have none
regarding North Sea herring. The Chief Executive of the Federation
has said that the decision would be received by the Scottish
fishermen with absolute fury."

As the bulk of the fisheries and the fleets are in Scottish waters
I ask that you issue instructions for the administration of these
licences to be transferred from the Ministry of Agriculture in
London to the Department of Agriculture in the Scottish Office.

Yours sincerely,

Donald Stewart

10 DOWNING STREET

8 July 1985

Dear Mr. Stewart

    Thank you for your letter of 18 June about mackerel
licences. Of course it is regrettable that such licences
should have been issued by the Ministry of Agriculture,
Fisheries and Food to freezer trawlers new to the fishery
which did not meet the detailed conditions of eligibility
originally determined in 1980. I understand however that
circumstances in the pelagic fisheries, including the
structure of the fleet, have changed sufficiently since 1980
for the Fisheries Ministers, including the Secretary of
State for Scotland, to have agreed that a review of the
restrictive licensing arrangements for these fisheries would
be justified at this stage and that the licences issued as a
result of the misunderstanding can be allowed to stand on a
provisional basis, pending the outcome of the review.

    As to the question of North Sea herring, I understand
that about the time that the United Kingdom's then much
larger fleet of freezer trawlers was displaced from its main
distant water fishing grounds as a result of the general
extension of fishing limits to 200 miles, the North Sea
herring fishery was closed following severe over-fishing.
Given the drastic reduction in the freezer trawler sector by
1983 when the fishery was reopened, initially on a limited
basis, it is difficult to draw any great conclusion from the
lack of any "historical presence" of freezer trawlers in the
fishery. It would in any case seem inappropriate to
restrict access to the developing North Sea herring fishery

more narrowly than to other pelagic fisheries. The
management arrangements for this year's fishery are I
understand to be the subject of consultation with the
interested industry organisations very shortly.

While I can understand the strong feelings of Scottish
fishermen on this matter, which have no doubt led to the
suggestion in the last paragraph of your letter for a change
of departmental responsibility, I do assure you that it is
the Government's aim to pursue a single policy for all parts
of the United Kingdom fishing fleet both within British
fishing limits and in other waters open to us under the
Common Fisheries Policy of the European Community. Although
misunderstandings like the one in question can, and
regrettably do, occasionally occur, I do not think that this
amounts to a sufficient reason for centralising the
administration of fisheries licensing arrangements in one
Department, contrary to successive Governments' previous
practice.

Yours sincerely

Margaret Thatcher

The Rt. Hon. Donald Stewart, M.P.

I look back with some satisfaction to my contribution in the Commons in defending the fishing industry. I was greatly honoured in 1987 to be presented with an inscribed crystal bowl from the Chairman and Members of the Mallaig and North-West Fishermen's Association. It has a proud place in our home.

9: THE FALKLANDS CONFLICT

The Seventies brought an escalation of the pressure by Argentina for the return to their sovereignty of the Falkland Islands, in their terminology, the Malvinas. The islanders had never expressed a desire to be taken over by Argentina and indeed were strongly opposed to the idea. Until the time came, if it ever did, that residents made known their wish for absorption, an all-party group in the Commons was determined to support their attitude. From time to time the Group met islanders visiting the UK and so kept abreast of developments, as well as demanding regular reports from Foreign Office ministers on discussions with Argentine representatives. With a view to improving communications, members of the Group pressed repeatedly for the construction of an air field in the islands and just as regularly the Government gave this the thumbs down.

On Friday, April 2, 1982, rumours began to circulate in the House that an invasion of the islands by Argentina was under way. Humphrey Atkins, the Lord Privy Seal, was unable to confirm this to the Commons. (It was reported some days later that the first indication that the story was true came from a radio ham in the north of England who had been in touch with a contact in the Falklands.)

For the first time in over twenty years the House was recalled on a Saturday for an emergency debate. The atmosphere in the Chamber was tense. Owing to the lack of specific information, there was a degree of confusion as well.

The Prime Minister, Mrs. Thatcher, opened the debate, outlining the background of events as far as they were known, and in the course of her speech spelt out in three sentences the stance her Government would adopt:

> I must tell the House that the Falkland Islands and their dependencies remain British territory. No aggression and no invasion can alter that simple fact. It is the Government's objective to see that the islands are freed from occupation and are returned to British administration at the earliest possible moment.

I had no quarrel with this standpoint.

In the early days of the conflict the words and bearing of the Prime Minister reflected the gravity of the situation and its potential dangers. When it was over she became triumphalist and jingoistic: "People who had secret fears that Britain was no longer the nation that had built an empire and ruled a quarter of the world. Well, they are wrong."

Because of the Scottish connection with the Falklands, and particularly the Highlands and Islands, I had joined the Falkland Islands Association shortly after my arrival at Westminster. The aim of the Association was to defend and advance the interests of the islanders, and the time had arrived when these interests were at stake.

Following a vote, the time allotted to the debate was three hours. I was fortunate to be called and in my brief contribution I said:

> It is clear that there has been a lack of intelligence, information and preparedness but . . . this is not the time to go into that. The fact remains that for many years successive governments have given the people of the Falklands an assurance that their interests would be protected. They are entitled to the right of self-

46

determination, and they have said quite clearly that they have no wish to be taken under the wing of the Argentine. I hope that this matter can be resolved without force, but if force is necessary, so be it.

The debate revealed almost total unanimity for resisting the Argentine aggression, the few dissident voices shown to be out of step with the sense of outrage felt by the House. The Task Force was assembled and despatched and the war took its course with casualties on both sides.

While efforts to expel the Argentinians were under way, on two occasions I had meetings with the Prime Minister. The only others present were Ian Gow, her PPS, later tragically murdered by the IRA, and Willie Whitelaw on the second occasion. With the outcome still in the balance, she was serious and concerned. I was satisfied, and this was confirmed by subsequent events, that she had given me a frank appraisal and accurate information.

Needless to say, the war dominated all other matters in the House. I recall the shock and tragedy of the loss of HMS *Sheffield.* There were statements and questions daily and one issue which some Members wished to pursue was the sinking of the Argentine cruiser, the *Belgrano,* on the grounds that "the ship was steaming away from the Task Force," "it was an illegal act," etc. To my mind, this type of charge was nonsense since Argentina was guilty of aggression and so her armed forces were all legitimate targets.

The outcome of the war turned out to be a triumph for Mrs. Thatcher and she milked it for all it was worth. In fact, despite the white-wash of the Franks Report some months later, her Government bore some responsibility for the Argentine attack, since the withdrawal of HMS

Endurance had signalled to Argentina a lack of commitment by the British Government to the Falklands. (In 1977, when the Junta were making aggressive noises about the Falklands, the Foreign Secretary, James Callaghan, arranged for the despatch of a nuclear submarine and two frigates to the South Atlantic. This hint was taken on board by Argentina.) Another item which was shoved under the carpet was the intention of the Thatcher Government to introduce legislation which would have deprived 400 Falkland Islanders of British citizenship. It hardly chimed with her declaration that 'the interests of the islanders are paramount'.

The Franks Report of January 1983 listed a number of issues on which Labour and Tory governments were guilty of negligence or indifference towards the Falklands but concluded that the Government did not bear the responsibility for the war. In the House I spoke in disagreement with this verdict but this did not affect, then or subsequently, my view that the expulsion of the Argentines from the islands was a course of action which was unavoidable. Whether a Fortress Falklands stretching into the future is tenable, only sober judgment in the Islands and the British and Argentine governments can decide.

10: THE COMMON MARKET

The Common Market or the European Economic Community (EEC) has now become the EC; the pretence, therefore,that it is purely an economic arrangement has now been abandoned. There was some merit in the original intention to merge coal and steel interests in certain European countries, but the appetite grew and the current monster shows no sign of being satiated.

It is unlikely that any confidence trick in history exceeded the scale of the pressure for forcing the United Kingdom into membership of the EEC. In the early days of the propaganda barrage, an enquirer seeking information on the political aspect would be directed to 'think of the economic gains' and, if the potential economic gains were queried, then the important issue to consider became 'the political advantages of a united Europe'. The latter was based, presumably, on the doubtful premise that without integration the French and the Germans would have been again at each other's throats. There is no evidence to sustain this theory and it is worth noting that, on other occasions, the same people would ascribe the years of peace since 1945 to NATO or the nuclear deterrent.

As an ex-serviceman I felt it went against my grain to cast off countries such as New Zealand, Australia and Canada, who had stood by us in the two German wars, to line up with continental countries, some of whom had been in the enemy camp. It also seemed illogical (to put it mildly) for a Nationalist striving to regain power for the people of

Scotland, to hand over power to a faceless European bureaucracy.

The enthusiasm of the pro-marketeers in the House of Commons in advocating total submersion of the U.K. in the EEC, both prior to and following the signing of the Treaty of Rome, was almost beyond belief. The directives and aims of the EEC, they argued, should not be questioned and should be swallowed even in disregard of their own country's interests, although, of course, they did not make the case in these terms.

Edward Heath, Prime Minister at the time, had made the specific undertaking that his intention was to negotiate 'no more and no less' and had given repeated assurances that British entry would take place only with 'the full-hearted consent of Parliament and people'. The fait accompli with which the country was presented was a blatant betrayal of these commitments. That is why, in his demotion and subsequent shunting aside, I always felt he had it coming to him.

One of the more ludicrous aspects of Heath's scenario for British entry was the prospect of 'going in to provide leadership in Europe'. It was taken up by his supporters in their unthinking acceptance of British superiority as if the French and the Germans would move aside to allow a Johnny-come-lately to join a club fifteen years after its establishment and proceed to run it.

Among the carrots dangled before the British public was the vision of an enormous new market eager to snap up the export capacity of the UK. In actual fact, it had the opposite result. In 1970, UK trade in manufactures with the EEC was in surplus – a small surplus, it is true, but by 1989 we had a trade deficit with the EEC of £13.6 billion.

As an example of the starry-eyed optimism of pro-marketeers I quote an incident with Lord Stokes, then Chairman of the British Leyland Motor Corporation. He wrote to Members of Parliament in 1971 pointing out that his company had been strongly in favour of British membership of the EEC ever since it had become an issue. He ended his letter saying that "as the country's largest individual exporter, we see immense opportunities for us in the EEC and we are eager to take advantage of them."

I replied to his Lordship, reminding him that Scotland had entered a common market with England in 1707 from which we had never recovered. I went on to say:

> If the present negotiations are successful, I will be able to watch Britain going through the process of losing control over her own affairs.
> The reference to 1707 may appear to you to be ancient history but I would say that your industry will be stamped into the ground by your continental competitors . . . If Britain enters the Common Market the removal of tariffs will give rise to a flood of continental cars into Britain and not the other way about.

Lord Stokes replied promptly saying:

> If all tariff barriers on both sides are removed we are quite confident that, on the basis of the rise in our sales in Europe to date, the major restructuring which is taking place in our European sales and manufacturing organisations, and the results of our market research in Continental markets, we as a company will gain far more than we will lose to Continental competition in the UK.
> As a matter of interest, our own sales in Europe are greater than those of all Continental manufacturers

combined in the UK. For this reason, we are quite confident that we will not prove to be the Scotland of the Common Market.

I rest my case by pointing out that in 1972 imports took 15% of the U.K. car market, and now they take close to 60%.

The lunacy of the Common Agricultural Policy (CAP) is widely recognised. Its disastrous effects include inflated food prices, prairie farming, stock-piling of food (much of it sold at give-away prices to the former Soviet Union and even to Libya) and the destruction of food and plants. All attempts at reforming the CAP in any meaningful way have failed and the pressure of Continental farmers on politicians will ensure that they will always fail.

Fraud in the EEC is on an enormous scale, such as is evidenced by the claims of Italian farmers for compensation for tomato plants which have never existed. Even crazier are the 'legal' fiddles embarked on to qualify for subsidies. I drew attention in the House of Commons to a cargo of rice which was loaded on a vessel in Holland, taken to Glasgow, off-loaded, then re-loaded and despatched to Germany. The same cargo in the same ship at each stage! The Ministry of Agriculture was not in the least put out. Apparently it's all in the game.

I had been in total opposition to membership of the EEC from the first indication of the British Government's intention to join. I spoke and voted accordingly, at all stages of the legislation as well as at meetings in Scotland and England as a member of the Anti-Common Market organisation. Watching how the EEC has developed since, I have no regrets and in fact I look back with satisfaction on campaigning for a 'No' vote in the Referendum, despite the final outcome. My constituency, the Western Isles, was the only one in the UK to vote against entry. In an editorial, the *Scotsman* expressed the view that the Isles vote was due to "the strong lead given by the Member of Parliament" but I suspect that, like the Norwegians, the people of the Isles were alive to the possible ruinous effects of EEC membership on the fishing industry.

The fears for the fishing industry have since been realised. As I am aware of the problems being faced by our fishermen, it saddens me to reflect that had we remained outside the EEC, our exclusive rights would extend to a 200 mile limit. What is even more tragic is that as I write, the European Court of Justice has ruled that British courts can freeze an Act of the Westminster Parliament while examining whether it fits in with EEC legislation, yet the House of Lords have found that British courts have no power to suspend an Act of Parliament.

The Act in question, The Merchant Shipping Act, was framed expressly to put an end to the loophole of registering Spanish fishing vessels as British to allow them access to British quotas of fish. The Act denied registration unless the boats were 75% in British ownership. This ruling by the European Court of Justice demonstrates the erosion of UK national sovereignty and loss of control of vital economic rights.

My attitude to the EEC has been criticised on the grounds that the Highlands and Islands have received considerable funding for local road-making, piers, etc. I have no intention, however, of saying 'Thank you' when I balance this against the fact that membership has meant that a family of four pays about £13.50 per week more for food; that UK taxpayers have already paid £12,000 million more to EEC institutions than they received back; that it has cost our fishermen control of waters up to a limit of 200 miles; and that, above all, decision-making on vital matters is being steadily diminished.

Incidentally, the British Government's 'clawback' policy has meant that substantial parts of the funding referred to above have been pocketed by the treasury. The grants are intended to be additional government allocations, but the European Parliament in 1987 declared:

> Few, if any, other governments go to the length of the UK government which makes pro-rata deductions from national allocations to infrastructure spending by local authorities when ERDF grants are made.

Lest these deductions be regarded as solely Tory Government fiddling, it should be borne in mind that from the inception of the Regional Fund in 1975 until it left office, the Labour Government initiated the clawback and, like other Labour innovations, it was maintained by the Tories.

The campaign in favour of UK membership of the EEC was unremitting and indeed unscrupulous. The arm-twisting of MPs took some amusing forms, such as the threat to a Tory that unless he voted 'Yes', action would be taken to see that he never again received an invitation to a Buckingham Palace garden party! During the voting which covered four days and nights, I would sometimes look up at the public gallery of the House and see the late Lord George-Brown gesticulating to his former Labour colleagues to get into the pro-market lobby.

For many of the Labour MPs his efforts were superfluous. Roy Jenkins and his acolytes were assiduous in their pro-market fervour, and it is a matter of note that in due course this group ended up by leaving the Labour Party to set up the Social Democratic Party. The pressure on individual Members was enormous and in the upshot, 69 Labour MPs voted for joining, with 19 abstaining.

In the early days of discussion, before the EEC legislation came on the Commons agenda, some Scottish Tories had told me of their opposition to the Market on such grounds as "selling out the Commonwealth" and "handing over our future to the Continentals". Alas, as time went on, they sensed how the wind was blowing and gradually announced their conversion to support of the concept. Teddy Taylor, to his credit, never wavered in his opposition, and is still battling to expose the myths of the alleged benefits of membership.

I became aware, as the debate went on, of an interesting sociological feature in individual attitudes to the Common Market among the Scottish Labour MPs. Those with professional backgrounds or an assured position, i.e. those who would survive comfortably whether Britain was in or out of the EEC, were pro-market. The genuine working-class representatives were almost all 'antis'.

To sum up, the desire to become part of the EEC appeared to me to be a realisation that the best days of the UK were over, and that it would be judicious to enter an eventide home. But it is beginning to get through to the British public that, despite assurances that no loss of sovereignty would be involved, they are step by step losing control over their own affairs and that, as the Delors plan indicates, the aim is integration. The EEC juggernaut is impelled by "the awful momentum that makes carrying through easier than cutting off a folly." (William Clark, *Glasgow Herald 14* June, 1985)

11: THE POLL TAX

Among the most stupid actions of the Thatcher regime, the introduction of the community charge or, as it more accurately became known, the poll tax, must take first place. The reaction of the greater majority of the British public was 'it shall not pass' and that's how it turned out.

The partial funding of local government by the rating system had long been a source of irritation, usually to the better-off. The excessively quoted example was the single pensioner living next door to the family with more than one source of income. Over a long period of time it had been SNP policy to replace rates with a local income tax.

All the same, it was nonsense for Tories to pretend that the country was seething with incipient revolution over the rating system. As a rough rule of thumb, one's accommodation bears relation to one's wealth or income. It is true that there were anomalies but despite its defects, it was still fairer than the poll tax proposed to replace it.

The decision to abolish rating was prompted by resistance to a proposed revaluation of properties in Scotland. The then Secretary of State for Scotland, George Younger, reacted to the howls of anguish from his Scottish supporters and it is believed that he played a considerable part in pushing the community charge. There were reasonable grounds for anger in that it would have been the second revaluation in Scotland without similar revaluation south of the border yet the cure prescribed was worse than the disease.

I submitted some of the objections in a debate on December 9, 1986, on the Abolition of Domestic Rates (Scotland) Bill. After stating the SNP position I went on:

> The per capita poll tax that we are discussing is even worse than the existing system. It hits hardest on the low-paid, even if there are rebates or exemptions for the unemployed. It is also highly impractical. How does the Government plan to take care of exemptions for periodic employment? How will registration be enforced without an army of officials, and how will payment be recovered from non-payers?

I think these points marked some of the main pitfalls of implementation of the legislation.

What set the heather on fire in Scotland was the role of guinea pigs assigned to the Scottish people. Some MPs who had voted, if not gleefully at least thoughtlessly, for the imposition of the tax on Scotland were in the vanguard of Doubting Thomases when England woke up to the implications. Lord Hailsham raised the question of the propriety of the House of Lords discussing a measure involving finance. No objection on these lines had been lodged by his Lordship or anyone else against the legislation covering Scotland.

The aim of the poll tax was to control expenditure from the centre and the public saw through the propaganda about accountability and issues such as strengthening democracy. In short, it lifted the lid from Thatcher's can of worms and many Tories shared in the rejoicing at its demise.

12: THE TORIES

In my first Parliament, 1970-1974, sitting on the Opposition benches, I was surrounded by Labour members and so it took longer to become acquainted with the Tories on the Government side. From sitting in the Chamber, however, it soon became apparent which Tories were men of weight, which were the NCOs, and which were the hacks and lobby fodder.

No matter how divergent their views from mine, I have always had a salute for the men of independent mind, the 'out of step', the thumbers-of-noses at Party brass. Needless to say, this attitude does not clash with the Party philosophy, and in fact these members are of greater worth to their party than the dull conformists, since they send a signal to the activists that men of integrity can survive within the party structure.

If a poll had been taken to pick the most respected Member of the Commons, the name of JOHN BIFFIN would be at or very near the top. A man of ability, with an unassuming demeanour, his speeches are models of humour and frankness which delight his audience. Boot-licking is foreign to his nature and even the wider public appreciates John Biffin as a man who 'tells it like it is'.

In the mid 1980s, John was Leader of the House and there was all-round approval for his handling of that function. On one occasion, when standing in for the Prime Minister, he rounded off his reply to a question from Dennis Skinner with the observation that "us grammar school boys must stick together"; an expression of comradeship which left Dennis Skinner speechless for once.

In talks with him during the Devolution debates, I found in John an understanding of the Scottish case which was rare among English Members. But John is an English nationalist and this also explains his neutrality towards the EEC. All round, an outstanding Member and a nice man.

The old-type Tories conformed to the obligations of the 'noblesse oblige' – the assumption that the better-off have a duty towards easing the lot of the less fortunate, or the tradition of the good officer looking after his men. There is something in the charge that this outlook is condescending and paternalistic but it is on a higher plane than the cut-throat Yuppiedom and jungle law that the Thatcher revolution set up. It was refreshing to find that many Tories remained faithful to the old landmarks.

Among the general public the name of SIR ROBERT RHODES JAMES would not spring instantly to mind as a prominent Member of the House. He is better known as the writer of stylish biographies, including those of Anthony Eden and Bob Boothby. Robert's interventions in debates were significant contributions to the issue and were not trimmed to meet the approval of the Party hierarchy or to play to the gallery.

NIGEL LAWSON can be numbered in the ranks of the unregimented as his resignation from office showed. The effects of his policies were calamitous. There must be some kind of hidden justice in the fact that an anagram of his name is WE ALL SIGN ON. He has a brusque manner and is not interested in running in the popularity stakes.

ANTHONY BEAUMONT-DARK typifies the Member who will not defend shabby or stupid actions even from his own side. He is quoted frequently in the Press, causing envious colleagues to mutter the 'rent-a-quote' charge, but one can understand the preference of newsmen for consulting Members who will express their views trenchantly and straightforwardly. He is also excellent company over a drink.

In the 1970s the most recognizable name among Scottish Tories, if not MPs of all parties, was TEDDY TAYLOR. He was a big fish in the Scottish pond – lined up, it was said, as Secretary of State for Scotland – until his defeat in Glasgow Cathcart. From there he departed to Southend on Sea and became one of a shoal of backbench minnows. He is still noteworthy for his powerful and consistent exposure of the myths about benefits from membership of the Common Market. Because it is delivered deadpan, many are unaware of his strongly developed sense of humour.

The late ALICK BUCHANAN-SMITH earned a high place in the regard of the Commons for decency and integrity. He was utterly trustworthy, and the tributes paid on his early and tragic death were statements of fact. A traditional Tory, he lived up to his ideal of public service. Knowing his views, it was no surprise when he resigned from the Tory Shadow Cabinet over the decision of the Conservative Party to oppose the Second Reading of the Devolution Bill. It was no surprise, either, that he kept his seat in 1987 when all the Tories about him were losing theirs.

In a piece I wrote some years ago, I said of Alick and Sir Hector Munro that Members like these could give the Tories a good name.

Other Tories are of note for less meritorious reasons than the names mentioned above.

MICHAEL HESELTINE (variously known as 'Goldilocks' or 'Tarzan') who is at the time of writing Secretary of State for the Environment, is a strangely unconvincing figure. I have always looked on him as a political spiv of the 'eyes blazing with insincerity' type. From the manner in which he set out to rubbish the CND, I agree with the *Observer* branding of him as 'an authoritarian demagogue'.

I stood only a few feet from him the night he seized and brandished the Mace. It was a rush of blood to the head that would remain impressed on the public mind. Thereafter when he rose to speak the Labour MP, ex-miner Tom Swain, would shout: "Pray silence for the Mace-bearer."

In spite of his precipitate resignation over the Westland Helicopter affair, he very quickly sent a signal of his fidelity to the Tory Party in the ensuing debate, in a speech which Gerald Kaufman described as "the unusual spectacle of a rat trying to rejoin a sinking ship."

Following Thatcher's downfall at the end of 1990, I was fairly certain that in the contest for the leadership Heseltine's chances of the succession to the Premiership were slim. Despite his popularity as a Tory Conference orator, he did not have a substantial base in the Party in the Commons. However, he deserves credit as the man who fired the first shot in the anti-Thatcher Revolution.

A founding member of Thatcherism and a stalwart defender of the Ark of the Thatcher Covenant, NICHOLAS RIDLEY (dubbed by a friend on the *Guardian* as 'Ridiculous Nidley'), chafed under the Heath Government's U-turns and had ready a blueprint for extensive privatisation long before Mrs. Thatcher had got into her stride privatising everything in sight.

The poll-tax fiasco, which he championed and defended against all attacks, knocked a large hole in his credibility. He finally fell through his indiscretions on the EC in a magazine. Though imprudent for a Cabinet Minister, his remarks on that subject, in my view, were accurate enough.

In the roulette of politics, it is not unknown for the disastrous speeches or actions to go past without repercussions while the fairly rational can bring doom in their wake.

In my first session in the Commons, Sir ALEC DOUGLAS-HOME was Foreign Secretary to the Heath Government. His was a tenure of Tory orthodoxy, as he went about spouting the slogans of the Cold War, supporting a Right-Wing stance and failing to take any initiative in disarmament plans.

As Lord Dunglass he had served as Neville Chamberlain's PPS and when Chamberlain's premiership was under threat, he made strong efforts to save Chamberlain even after the German invasion of Holland and France in 1940. In spite of this, his record as a Municheer had been forgotten, unlike that of 'Rab' Butler who was unable to shake off his Munich stance.

In the days of the Devolution debate, Sir Alec told the New York Caledonian Society that "the Scots know on which side their bread is buttered." This was offensive enough but almost irrelevant when placed alongside his action in advising Scottish voters to vote 'No' in the referendum on Devolution on the grounds that a better Bill would be brought forward. Not unexpectedly, such a Bill was never presented.

EDWINA CURRIE made no secret of her determination to be noticed. When attacked for some outrageous statement, she would grin broadly, savouring the thought that at least she was in the public eye. And it worked. She became the second best known woman in the House and went on to become a Minister.

From the time of her first appearance in the Commons, I had sensed that some day her tongue would get her into trouble. She caused offence by lecturing Northerners on their diet. (Tory ladies have an urge to instruct the workers on how to feed themselves. In the Depression in the thirties, Lady Astor proceeded to address a public meeting on a method of making soup from the heads of fish. She was brought up short by shouts of "who ate the fish?")

Mrs. Currie's 'foot in mouth' disease brought its punishment when she sounded off about the amount of salmonella in eggs. Since there was a good deal of substance in the charge, it is ironic that her fall should follow when she had done the state some service.

JOHN MACGREGOR, at the time of writing the Leader of the House, is a bland apologist for the Government action or lack of action. When pressed about, say, the shortage of teachers, his technique is to advise his questioner to "get it in perspective". He then reels off any positive aspects of policy, ending with "we are keeping it under review".

He is one of a number of Tory front-benchers whose elevation is difficult to justify. Among these I would name Tony Newton, Tom King, John Gummer, David Maclean,. and the unprepossessing Eric Forth, who, although himself a Scot, intervened at Scottish Question Time as the Member for an English seat, to attack the alleged feather-bedding of Scotland.

Putting aside political bias, an observer of the Tory and Labour front benches at the present time would conclude that the calibre of the Labour bench is superior. It seems as if Mrs. Thatcher had exhausted the supply of top stars and reduced the Tories to playing with a third eleven.

13: THE LABOUR PARTY

Running an eye over the current Labour Party and its policies, I cannot help, as a one-time member, being struck by the distance the party has travelled from the ideals and aims of Socialism, and the contrast with the idealism of past times.

It is hardly an exaggeration that the Tory-Labour battle is coming to resemble the Republican-Democrat struggle in the United States. When one considers the parallel objectives, the Presidential-style presentation of the leader and the personal attacks instead of policy differences, the similarity becomes clear. As the veteran Socialist, Lord Brockway said: "The Labour Party has tended to become a political contender for power, concerned about current issues within capitalism rather than a transformation of the basis of society." Or, as one of the down-to-earth Tories put it: "Any harm they will do will arise from wetness rather than redness."

It could be said of Attlee and Callaghan that their premierships – while hardly models of Socialist reconstruction – were consistent with their political record. The same could not be said of Wilson, who rose in the Labour Party through ostensibly left-wing credentials, moved quickly to the Right, and jettisoned, in the process, commitment to a Socialist society.

Even the most bitter opponents of the Tories must be asking themselves what kind of choice they have in voting for the Labour Party. We have watched on television Labour spokesmen rubbish the nationalisation principle more vehemently than the Tories, and, despite all the frenzied attacks during the passage of the privatisation Bills, we have seen no commitment by Labour to returning the plundered public assets to public ownership. So far has the sell-out of Socialism gone that Labour has supported the bailing out of Stock Exchange gamblers who had had a poor year at Lloyds after years of piling up profits.

In short, as Anthony Howard said, "If the red flag is flying today, it is flying over the tomb of Socialism."

Despite these strictures on the leadership of the Labour Party, it should be said in fairness, that the Party still has in its ranks men of worth and principle who adhere to the standards proclaimed as its aims and aspirations.

Such a man was ERIC HEFFER who died in 1991 after a long struggle with cancer and who occupied the time of his illness in writing four books. He was one of the old-fashioned Socialists, believing totally in the cause. He was portrayed in the right-wing press as a Bolshevik bogey-man, but he was in fact a Puritan, a firm advocate of democratic socialism, a libertarian and a tireless champion of the interests of the working class.

I had great respect and affection for Eric. One of the best-read men in the Commons, especially in Socialist theory and history, he enjoyed discussion and argument. Refusing to take a post in the Labour Government in the late 60s, he became a Minister of State at the Department of Trade and Industry in 1974 until he resigned over the Common Market the following year.

In speeches he could be harmlessly egotistical – "The whole nation knows of my interest in Italian politics" – and, as some of his obituarists noted, he had a short fuse,

Donald Steward and Gordon Wilson touring the Southern Isles in 1983.

Donald Stewart addressing the SNP Conference, 1978.

Photo: Gordon Wright Publishing

Donald and Chrissie Stewart meeting Her Majesty the Queen and Prince Philip in Stornoway.

Photo: Angus Smith Photographic

THE SNP "FIRST ELEVEN"

Left to right: Douglas Crawford, George Reid, Gordon Wilson, Douglas Henderson, Winnie Ewing, Donald Stewart, Margaret Ewing, Hamish Watt, Ian McCormack, Andrew Welsh, George Thopson.

Donald and Chrissie Stewart with Constituency Delegates at SNP Conference in Inverness

Donald and Chrissie Stewart on the ferry from Barra to Vatersay in 1985.

but would simmer down as quickly as he blew up. He would tell, with a rueful grin, stories against himself, as in the time he rose from his seat to storm out of the room at a meeting of the Labour group, to find in his grand gesture that the door he opened was the door of the broom cupboard. There was the occasion too, when the Labour M.P. Ron Brown was censured by the House for handling and dropping the Mace. Eric in protesting that the punishment recommended was too severe, was unable to complete a sentence which he began, "you don't take a sledgehammer to . . . ."

Another member in the same league is DENNIS SKINNER whose Socialist convictions are rock-fast and not merely a passport to future power on the Right of the party.

It is difficult to imagine the Commons chamber – day or night – without his presence. He refuses pairing, foreign trips, free meals and abhors absenteeism. So he is available to enter the lists against the enemy whatever the time or subject, and is a formidable opponent when he does so.

He had a part in shaking the confidence of Roy Jenkins on Roy's return to the House after winning the Glasgow-Hillhead by-election. While Dennis may not have originated the call "Silence for Jock" when Jenkins rose to his feet, he would shout "This is it!" when Roy would start a question to the Prime Minister, implying that Mrs. Thatcher was about to receive the coup-de-grace. When Roy's question turned out to be innocuous, Dennis would demand "Is that all?" implying that Roy had let us all down.

I was a witness to Nicholas Fairbairn's embarrassment at Dennis's hands: a condition in which Nicky was rarely found. On a budget day, Nicky appeared at the bar of the

House in tartan trews of a 'loud' pattern. On spotting this, Dennis called to the Speaker, "There's a man 'ere in his pyjamas, Mr. Speaker, he's 'ere in his pyjamas." Nicky reached into his pocket, produced a snuff-box and took a pinch, at which Dennis bellowed, "An 'e's on droogs an' all!"

When the diminutive Sports Minister, Colin Moynihan, planned to issue identity cards for football fans, Dennis declared, "It's all right for "im, he can go in through the cat flap." Another example of Dennis's wit, although it happened since my time in the Commons, was the lodging by some Tory MPs of an Early Day Motion congratulating Mrs. Thatcher on becoming a grandmother and wishing the new arrival well. An amendment appeared on the Order Paper the next day signed by Dennis in which he joined in the good wishes to the baby and hoped "he will learn to crawl as fast as the signatories to the above Motion."

The Labour Party – and the House of Commons – is not overburdened with Members of the wit and calibre of Dennis Skinner.

In the 1970s, a wind-up by MICHAEL FOOT would compensate for sitting through a day of turgid debate. The wit, the argument, the rhetoric were a delight, although sometimes he fell into the Roget Thesaurus style of oratory: "The EEC, the Common Market, the European Community – call it what you will."

Despite the robust attacking manner of his speeches, he is in private shy and restrained. That such a gentle, bookish individual, lacking in administrative ability, should have been chosen to lead the Labour Party was a monumental and costly error for them. Still, it pointed to the high place Michael held in the hearts of the majority of his fellow-members and to the intention of a section of the Labour Party to accept as leader anyone who wasn't Denis Healey.

It is a widely-held view, which I share, that in electoral terms the Labour Party would have travelled faster to power under the leadership of JOHN SMITH. [He was elected leader in 1992 - Ed.] He is an extremely able and industrious man (Michael Foot left most of the donkey work of the Scotland Bill to him), and a persuasive speaker with the skills of the trained advocate in not pushing his case higher than the evidence at hand can sustain. With a well-developed sense of humour, he is excellent company. All in all, a politician of a high standard and a nice man.

JACK ASHLEY holds a high place in the regard of colleagues in every part of the Commons. His courage in pursuing his career in the face of his severe disability of total deafness is nationally known, as are his unceasing campaigns for justice for the disabled and others to whom life has dealt a poor hand. As I tell elsewhere, I was privileged to introduce a Bill for the disabled which Jack had prepared.

On a number of occasions Jack has earned praise from Conservative opponents but has never allowed soft words to dull his critical faculties. He was unremitting in fighting for the disadvantaged of society who had in him their most concerned and effective champion.

I seldom found myself on the same wavelength as TAM DALYELL. We were on opposite sides on issues such as the Common Market, the Devolution Bill, nuclear power, the Falklands War, and, since my time in the House, the Gulf War.

He has numerous contacts in the old-school-tie network as befits a product of Eton and Cambridge and a past Chairman of the University Conservative Association.

Unlike the stance of Keir Hardie, who long ago declared that the working people of Scotland would never achieve their social aims so long as Scotland was subservient to English rule, Tam's opposition to Labour's Devolution proposals was persistent and tireless. He introduced the 'West Lothian Question' which highlighted the position of Scots MPs being able to participate in English affairs while English MPs could not influence the same matters in a Scottish Assembly. I cannot recall that he has taken much time in Parliament or space in the Press to protest against the devastation of Scotland by Thatcherism in defiance of the votes of the great majority of the Scottish people.

One of his anti-Assembly ploys was the threat that Scotland would be 'over-governed'. He reeled off community councils, district councils, regional councils, the Convention of Scottish Local Authorities, the Scottish Assembly, Westminster and Brussels. Apart from the fact that he was one of the Eurofanatics whose support lumbered us with the disastrous Brussels tier, and leaving aside the community councils and COSLA which are not governing bodies, and given that the SNP aim is to remove Westminster control, we are left with two bodies, or three if we are still in the EEC.

Tam was a great friend and confidant of Richard Crossman. It is a pity that he did not absorb Crossman's sound assessment that

> Nationalism is a necessary and creative concomitant
> of real popular liberty . . . Nationalism in fact, is an
> essential stage in the self-assertion and emancipation

of man. Nations .... are living organisms out of which individual freedom grows. Destroy the nation and you destroy freedom itself.

Occupying the leadership niche in the Labour Party in Scotland formerly held by Willie Ross is DONALD DEWAR, although Donald's control is, I suspect, less authoritarian. In debate he speaks too fast and often too long, but his contributions on the whole are rational and fair. He is inhibited, however, by the need to be seen as 'responsible' in that he cannot push the Tories too hard since he may be confronted with the same situation or circumstances when he delivers Scotland for the Labour Party. The United Kingdom comes first.

One of the funniest – and saddest – pointers to the Labour betrayal of Socialism was an item on a BBC news broadcast on March 6, 1992, which said: "The Conservatives have published a document showing the connection between Labour MPs and left-wing causes. The opposition has denounced this as a smear campaign."

14: THE LIBERALS AND THE SOCIAL DEMOCRATS

'To break the mould of British politics' was the avowed aim at the formation of the Social Democratic Party. It was a worthy objective in the light of the existing fossil remains of the Conservative and Labour parties, but unfortunately they blew it and proceeded on the old paths, even to the length of fission. At that stage they fully deserved Michael Foot's comment: "The SDP isn't quite what it was. And it wasn't much, was it, even then?"

The founding Gang of Four – Roy Jenkins, William Rodgers, Dr. David Owen and Shirley Williams – were politicians who shared, among other views, one over-riding commitment; they were Euro-fanatics, serving notice that if the new party had any idea of withdrawal from the EEC, they would promptly depart. This fitted in with the line of their Liberal partners in the Alliance.

Before the secession of the SDP Members from the Labour Party, I had often wondered, in the light of the policies and the professed ideals of Labour, how they managed to remain on board. None was likely to intend any harm to the capitalist system, although the establishment of a Socialist society was the great motivating force which kept the activists in the Labour Party working. I should add in passing that this does not imply that the Labour MPs who stayed put are fired by the spirit of Bolshevism.

It is remarkable, in the light of his later actions, that it was David Steel who advised Roy Jenkins in the early moves, that a separate party would be preferable to the disaffected Labourites joining the Liberal Party. Before the break, Shirley Williams (whom I had always regarded as a much over-rated politician) had stigmatised a centre party as having "no roots, no principles, no philosophy and no values."

Anyway, in the end they did form a new party, and it appeared to fill a vacuum on the British political scene. I could not see its relevance to Scotland in view of evidence from Barbara Castle's Diaries that Roy Jenkins and Shirley Williams were among the foremost opponents in the Labour Cabinet of Devolution for Scotland. There was also William Rodger's assertion that the SDP would be "a party for the whole of England." I must concede, however, that the SDP programme gave Scottish government some priority and certainly Dr. David Owen was a strong advocate of this line.

It was the same David Steel who jumped the gun on the question of a merger between the Liberals and the SDP. David Owen had at least indicated the need to proceed slowly with amalgamation and his refusal to be conscripted for the new set-up was understandable. The document outlining the policies to be followed by the new party (later known as 'the dead parrot') cobbled up by Steel and Robert Maclennan almost scuppered both wings on the spot. Under pressure from other Members, it was promptly repudiated by the authors but it shattered the credibility of the Social and Liberal Democrats to a degree from which they have not recovered. It was a monumental error on Steel's part, and the verdict on the SDP and the Liberals would be, as the poet said of the First World War general and the two soldiers, "he did for them both with his plan of attack."

The earlier Liberal Party was a considerable force in the Commons. Led by the redoubtable Jo Grimond (later Lord Grimond), there were periods when it looked as if its time had come. It was particularly frustrating for them in the February 1974 Election when, by then under Jeremy Thorpe's leadership, they had votes to the extent of more than half the votes cast for the Conservative and Labour parties. They ended up, as a result of the unfair voting system of the UK, with only a handful of seats.

Reverting to Mr. Grimond, I always regarded him as a man of obvious leadership timber who would have occupied top rank in either of the so-called major parties.

Despite a long-standing commitment to Scottish government in the Liberal programme, their Parliamentary party never appeared to me to give the issue any priority. David Steel clearly wished to act as a British politician and, the Devolution Bill apart, I cannot recall his getting worked up over Scottish affairs. Labour Members such as Dennis Canavan and David Lambie were keener champions of Scottish interests.

The Liberal and Social Democrats include in their Commons number several MPs of high quality. The well-respected Sir Russell Johnston can always be depended on to speak for civilised and libertarian values, though I disagree totally with his commitment to the EEC. Alan Beith, Malcolm Bruce and Charles Kennedy would be assets in any party. The latter, despite having to live down a 'baby of the House' tag, quickly showed his maturity and skill in debate. The Welshman, Geraint Howells, who confines himself mainly to debates on agricultural subjects, is the best type of old-style Liberal.

Like the SNP, the Social and Liberal Democrats are regarded by the Tory and Labour parties as interlopers who should not be in the game. It has not gone unnoticed that in numerous by-elections, Tories would prefer to lose to Labour, and Labour, if unsuccessful, would prefer that a Tory win rather than that the victor should come from – in their terminology – the minor parties. The Liberal Democrats have a role in the Commons which is useful against the big battalions. As I write, however, the times are not propitious for them to increase until a fairer voting system is in place and that is their 'Catch 22' situation.

15: THE HOUSE OF LORDS

At a time when the House of Lords were voting against and even defeating Tory Government Bills, Lord Blyton (ex-miner and Labour MP) was heard to chortle, "I don't hear our lot talking so loudly now about abolishing the Lords."

The Labour Party has blown hot and cold on the issue. They huff and they puff but they don't bring the House down. Their attitude – that a revising chamber is not needed – will have the effect of ensuring that the House of Lords will have a permanent existence since nearly all democracies have a second chamber. Harold Wilson boasted that he had always accepted Heath's and Thorpe's nominees for peerages and knighthoods; so it's a cosy Establishment racket with Tory, Labour and Liberal (now Democrat) involvement.

In its present, i.e. non-elective form, the House of Lords is an offence against democracy. It is a salutary exercise to cast one's eye over the list of their Lordships and to ask oneself, "What contribution to the welfare and advance of the nation justifies each one his place in the Lords?" It has, of course, a built-in Tory majority, as was shown in the poll-tax debate in 1989 when backwoodsmen who never appear in the House were shepherded through the voting lobbies to clinch a Government majority on the Bill. On that occasion, one of their number signed the register for the first time!

Presumably on the grounds that nothing succeeds like failure, defeat at the polls is a not infrequent mode of entry to the Lords. The Tory M.P. Hamish Gray, who was sent packing by his Ross and Cromarty constituents, surfaced in a few days by being translated to the House of Lords as Lord Gray of Contin. This action of Thatcher's outraged democracy, not to mention Highlanders. The offence was compounded by Lord Gray being appointed at the same time to the Scottish Office as Minister responsible for the Highlands and Islands!

Mrs. Thatcher used patronage on a massive scale. By 1987 she had appointed 123 new peers and by the time she resigned the number must have been over 200.

It goes without saying that the House of Lords contains a fair proportion of eccentrics. One noble Lord had the fairly sensible hobby of tying salmon flies, but was perhaps a bit unusual in putting his head below the surface of his bath-water to see how they might look to a fish. Another departure from orthodoxy was Lord Avebury's announced intention to leave his body to a dogs' home. I greatly enjoyed the headline in the *Scotsman:* "Dogs' Home to get pedigree chum."

The late Lord Arran successfully piloted through the Lords a Bill to protect homosexuals. A year or two later he submitted a Bill for the protection of badgers but the support on this occasion was poor. On this being pointed out by a colleague his Lordship remarked ruefully, "There are very few badgers in the House of Lords."

In a ballot one year for Private Member's Bills, my name came near the top which implied that my choice of subject would have a chance of being debated. As happens in these circumstances, one is bombarded with suggestions for the object the Bill should seek to achieve. One of their Lordships wrote to me proposing that my Bill should be legislation to maintain the Prayer Book of the Church of

England, this being a current issue in that Church. It did not take me long to imagine the outcry if Church of England services were to be tampered with by a Free Church of Scotland adherent and a Member of Parliament for the SNP. I was obliged to reject the carrot which he dangled before me as a reward: a promise that my name would appear in an editorial in the *Daily Telegraph*.

Up until now, no members of the Scottish National Party have been nominated for a seat in the House of Lords, although I have heard views from time to time that the Party should be represented there. After the 1983 General Election, the *Sunday Post* ran a story that "the veteran SNP MP Donald Stewart" was being considered as likely to go to the Lords. This led to SNP Headquarters receiving mail asking whether this was accurate, and on the advice of an office-bearer of the Party, I took the chance of making it clear in a speech to Conference that if such an offer were made, it would not be accepted by me.

My opposition to SNP members sitting in the Lords is based on the fact that (1) as stated above, the House of Lords as it exists is totally undemocratic; (2) SNP representation would put the Party firmly in the British Establishment; and (3) it would suggest that an SNP presence would be a permanent feature of the British Parliament.

A decision by the Scottish National Party to accept the offer of a Lords seat will signify that the Party has opted for squatting in a British lay-by in preference to advancing along the road to Scottish independence. Of course, it is all academic. I do not believe that a Tory government will give the matter a second's consideration.

16: THE SPEAKERS

In my time in the Commons I sat under four speakers. Although they were four very different individuals, I can say of them all that they honoured the long-standing convention of the House that all points of view must be heard, and even in my time as a one-man Party, I never had reason to complain that treatment of me was other than scrupulously fair.

After 1974, as a Party leader, and subsequently on my appointment to the Privy Council, I found it became easier to get called upon to speak. Of course, Members who are not Privy Councillors resent the priority afforded to PCs in debate. This grousing ceases when they are admitted to the Privy Council.

HORACE KING

On my arrival at Westminster in 1970 the Chair was occupied by Dr. Horace King (later Lord Mowbray-King). He was the first holder of the office from the Labour Party. In the early 70s the House was fairly tame due to the shattering of Harold Wilson from his totally unexpected defeat in the General Election and the Tories having suffered a severe setback by the death of Ian Macleod a few weeks after the election. I do not recall that Dr. King had any great difficulty in exercising his authority.

SELWYN LLOYD

On his retirement in 1971, Dr. King was followed by Selwyn Lloyd, Q.C., who had filled high Cabinet posts including those of Foreign Secretary and Chancellor of the Exchequer. He had been a victim of Harold Macmillan's 'Night of the long knives' when seven members of the Cabinet had been sacked. No doubt the blow was painful; he had done the state and the Tory Party some service, particularly in keeping to himself the full story of the Suez adventure. However, Alec Douglas-Home brought him back as Leader of the House. I have been told by colleagues at the time that he was extremely effective in this job which may have laid the foundations for his election in due course to the Speakership.

Selwyn Lloyd was an excellent straight-down-the-middle Speaker. An indication of his authority in the House is the fact that no Member was 'named' during his time in the Chair. Speaking for myself, I can say that I always found him fair, courteous and helpful.

Privately, he was full of humour and laughed a great deal as he spoke, but this side of him was not often seen in the House. I recall a Labour Member rising to ask him for advice "not as Speaker but as a lawyer". Selwyn bounded to his feet to tell the Honourable Gentleman that anyone demanding free advice from a lawyer would find it worth exactly what he paid for it.

When valedictory speeches were made on the occasion of his retirement from the Chair, I included in my remarks a reference to his term as Chairman of the Services Committee of the House and how he had been most assiduous in improving facilities and conditions for

Members. He wrote me a note the next day expressing his grateful thanks for my stressing his efforts in this direction.

GEORGE THOMAS

George Thomas was the best all-round Speaker in my time. A friendly, warm-hearted, gregarious man, he had to accept the isolation of the office which cut him off from activities he enjoyed such as chaffing and swopping stories in the tea-room, but he compensated for it to some extent by having guests for dinner in his apartments in the House. It is likely that the Speaker's House had never before seen such frequent dinner parties. Chrissie and I were recipients of his hospitality on a number of occasions.

One of these occasions was a party for all the Party leaders and their wives. It was certainly an innovation to arrange this and there was complete agreement that it had worked. Harold Wilson was Prime Minister and he dominated the conversation both at the table and afterwards in his egocentric fashion. All the same, it was a unique experience and I have wondered whether it has been repeated since.

We were guests again of Speaker Thomas on the night of May 4, 1977. The previous day, both Houses of Parliament had met in Westminster Hall to mark the Queen's 25 years on the throne. In her reply to the addresses from the Lord Chancellor and the Speaker, the Queen included a comment on the lines that she hadn't become Queen to preside over the break-up of the United Kingdom. This was clearly aimed at the then current Nationalist fervour in Scotland and Wales. At the end of the proceedings I was confronted at the door of the Hall by Stewart Trotter of the *Glasgow Herald* and Tom James of the *Scotsman,* who asked for my reaction to the passage mentioned. I said that recognition of the Crown as Head of the Commonwealth was SNP policy and that we were happy to continue this after independence, but that if we were forced to choose between the Monarchy and independence, we would choose independence. This statement, needless to say, received considerable publicity. But at the dinner that night, when the Speaker introduced me, I thought H.M. showed more than usual interest when he mentioned my name, although she gave no sign of sending me to the Tower!

George Thomas says in his autobiography that, following the news of Selwyn Lloyd's pending retirement, I was the first Party leader to let him know of my Party's support for his election as Speaker. Politically, I was opposed to his views on Devolution for Wales on which he took the hard-line 'United Kingdom' position. He was proud to be 'British' and was severely critical of Plaid Cymru.

Nevertheless, we had come to the conclusion that he was a fair man and that his record as Deputy Speaker indicated that he would fill the office adequately. As it turned out, this view was shared throughout the House. He became an outstanding occupant of the Chair and, to the surprise of some who had thought he was too easy-going to keep order, he was a firm Speaker who kept control of the House. From the SNP standpoint – despite his anti-Nationalist attitude as an MP – we always received fair consideration. There were mutterings from some Labour quarters that he was too partial to the Tories, but it seems to be the fate of Speakers to be regarded with suspicion by their erstwhile colleagues.

His great asset in the Chair was his sense of humour and his ready wit. I recall a Tory Member referring to the proceedings of a Select Committee. Bob Hughes (Lab. Aberdeen N.) shouted across the floor, "It hasn't reported yet, you twit!" Speaker Thomas, looking directly at Bob, commented, "The Honourable Gentleman has taken the words right out of my mouth." The idea of the Speaker rebuking a Member in these terms convulsed the House.

Another Member, pressing for instant debate on some topical issue ended his plea by pointing out, "It was in today's paper, Mr. Speaker."

"So was my horoscope," rejoined George, "and it wasn't any more accurate."

His facility to reduce tension by these means was evident when an English Member was offensive about the accent of my colleague Winnie Ewing. She promptly protested to the Speaker. He rose to his feet and declared in a heavy Welsh accent: "There are a lot of accents in this House; makes me wish I had one myself." The storm subsided in laughter in which Winnie joined.

BERNARD WEATHERILL

Speaker Weatherill, known to his friends as Jack, was elected to the Chair in 1983. It was widely whispered that Mrs. Thatcher's choice to follow George Thomas was Humphrey Atkins. Although I did not detect any personal animosity to Atkins, the House or at least the senior Members were determined that Mrs. Thatcher would not be allowed to dictate the choice of Speaker and the well-respected Weatherill was duly elevated.

Jack Weatherill is a qualified tailor although his position in that industry is somewhat higher than these words imply, as he was Managing Director of a famous family business. He keeps a thimble in a waistcoat pocket as a reminder of his origins and to guard against a swollen head – although to anyone who knows him the danger is slight.

He very quickly demonstrated that he was the servant of the House and not an instrument for ensuring an easy passage for Government business. This, for example, is borne out by the number of Private Notice Questions which he has allowed. These are usually initiated by the Opposition on issues which the Government would prefer to keep under wraps. For this, he was not a favourite of the Thatcher administration.

Another of his qualities, as I see it, is that he is not unduly exercised over robust confrontation in the House. He recognizes that the political game is sometimes rough and that the layout and history of the Commons Chamber properly provides an arena for differing views to be vigorously expounded.

As I write, it occurs to me that I do not recall Jack Weatherill making a speech in the House. No doubt he had done so in his early years, but by the time of my arrival he had been made a Whip, which places the holder under an obligation to refrain from speaking. So the non-speaker became the Speaker.

17: PRIME MINISTERS

HAROLD WILSON

When I entered the Commons Chamber for the first time, Harold Wilson sat on the Opposition front bench. Little of the dynamism so prominent in his past rhetoric was apparent, as it emerged that the result of the 1970 General Election had left him shattered. He had strolled around the country in a lack-lustre, low-profile campaign, acting the statesman above the sordid squabbling, in the full expectation that no removal vans would be calling at No. 10 Downing Street.

In the four years of the Heath Government, I do not recall having any conversation with Wilson. Early in 1974, after the Labour victory in the February election, Douglas Henderson, our Party Whip, asked for a meeting with him to ascertain his views on Scottish Devolution. We met the Prime Minister in his office and the discussion was relaxed and agreeable enough. At a Press Gallery lunch two years later, I was amused to hear Harold tell the Press that the Labour Party had criticised him for having talks with the Leader of the SNP! This says something for Harold's memory and how he could 'hype up' events.

In dealing with opponents he was fast on his feet. Once, Prime Minister's Questions fell on the anniversary of Bannockburn, and in putting some Scottish point of moment to him, I referred in passing to "a fight between the English and Scots in 1314 where certain satisfactory conclusions were reached." He promptly advised me to read up on the battle of Pinkie where the boot had been on the other foot. I gave him full marks mentally as few Scots even would have had that piece of history on immediate recall.

There was one famous episode where he had been wrong-footed. In the 60s, speaking at an Election meeting in Chatham, he was unwise enough to pose the question: "Why do I emphasise the role of the Navy?" A voice that said "because you're speaking in Chatham" put an end to his musing.

Another time, deflecting an attack by Winnie Ewing, he told her: "At the airport on my last visit I saw some of your supporters, cheerful and enthusiastic, whose only contribution was to hold the flag of Scotland upside down." Needless to say, this riposte tickled the Labour groundlings, but it was smart-alec nonsense since the St. Andrews flag, unlike the Union flag, is symmetrical and so is the same either way.

"A week is a long time in politics," he once stated. His record of short-term political ends, his changes of policies and constant announcements of new initiatives (which seldom got off the drawing board) demonstrated his belief in that dictum. The much-vaunted National Plan died shortly after birth; the reform of the House of Lords didn't get very far; the Ombudsman was appointed but with powers inferior to the need; and a Minister for Disarmament was installed to be followed a few weeks later with the appointment of a salesman to sell British armaments abroad!

A great provider of sustenance for the Press in the way of news, he found that his honeymoon with them came to an end once the papers had latched on to the consistent non-performance of his government. From then on there were regular hints of Press conspiracies and of Tory journalists prospecting for anti-Labour dirt. (Unlike Attlee, who, when told that the following day's *Times* would carry a virulent attack on him, murmured, "That so? Circulation falling, d'ye think?")

Labour had hoped that his return to power in 1974 would correct the errors of the 1964-70 period of office which they regarded as a disaster. But he resigned after two years, handing the shop over to James Callaghan just before the roof fell in. Incidentally, I have been asked frequently what was behind his resignation. I know of nothing by way of explanation; the then Speaker, George Thomas, assured me that Wilson had confided in him several months earlier that he would go the following March.

Historians, I feel sure, will not deal kindly with Harold Wilson and his terms of office as Prime Minister. So much promise, so little performance (or performance of the wrong kind). He is summed up for me when I hear or read a reference to Lord Home's devastating return volley to Wilson's branding him as "the 14th Earl".

"I suppose," said Sir Alec (as he was then), "that means he's the 14th Mr. Wilson."

JAMES CALLAGHAN

Without hesitation I would place James Callaghan (now Lord Callaghan) as the best Prime Minister in my experience in the House of Commons. I make this judgment on several counts: on the basis of his commitment to raising the conditions of the under-privileged in society, his robust common sense, his political experience which provided him with sensitive antennae and his innate decency.

In a piece which I wrote for the *Glasgow Herald* in March I said:

> Compared with the great fixer Harold Wilson, the present Prime Minister appears to be a less able occupant of Number 10. I believe he has been seriously under-estimated in some quarters. He has considerable ability in leadership, more honesty in facing and admitting awkward facts and, without alienating his left-wing, projects an image as a consensus politician capable of healing wounds.

It was his misfortune that he entered Downing Street at a moment of maximum difficulty, with the economy in crisis and pay policy in a shambles. To cap it all, his majority in Parliament was unreliable to say the least. Nevertheless, he soldiered on, and had not the 'winter of discontent' intervened, would have established himself as an outstanding Prime Minister.

In the Chamber he gave an impression of imperturbability, of a sure hand on the tiller. He could handle Margaret Thatcher superbly. She invariably emerged from a bout with Jim in a bruised condition. The image was of a spoiled, bad-tempered little girl trying to kick the shins of an amused and restraining adult. (Kinnock's subsequent efforts with her at Prime Minister's Questions brought to mind the phrase "sending a boy to do a man's work.")

I had a meeting with him in his office the evening prior to the censure debate which ended the life of the government. Nobody else was present and we had a friendly talk in which he appeared relaxed and even fatalistic as I made clear the intention of the SNP to vote against the government unless the Scotland Bill was submitted on a vote of confidence basis. He made no effort of begging us to call off. Presumably he had realized that it would not be possible to dragoon the rabid anti-devolutionists in the Labour Party into supporting their own government's legislation. And he may have sensed that the die was cast.

In another *Glasgow Herald* article some months earlier (19 Jan. 1979) I had made the forecast:

> There is widespread resentment at the present wave of strikes and with a General Election a few months away at most, the unions may have ensured the return of a Tory government at Westminster, in spite of Mrs. Thatcher's leadership which had made it look increasingly unlikely. The unions may have delivered Uncle Jim into her hands.

I certainly got that one bang on.

After his retirement from the leadership of the Labour Party, he chose to sit on the bench I occupied. I was able to enjoy his shrewd and tolerant observations on the business and personalities of the House. His long and varied experience – he had served as Home Secretary, Foreign Secretary and Chancellor of the Exchequer – was unique and his acquaintance with world leaders was wide. He is a man of stature for whom I have the greatest respect.

MARGARET THATCHER

Apart from the row over the removing of entitlement to school milk from children, I was hardly aware of Mrs. Thatcher prior to her election as leader of the Tory Party. Since coming to power in the General Election of 1979 she has impinged on all citizens of the UK and, except for the well-heeled, in a manner seldom to their approval.

Most of the claims for advances made under her administration are bogus. True, unemployment figures have been dropping, but only from the astronomical heights to which she pushed them in the early 1980s. The corner shop philosophy of putting a nest egg aside, paying your bills, living within your means, etc., has ended up with an uncontrolled spending spree of overdrafts, crippling mortgages and credit card debt run riot, and so on.

In spite of 'law and order' objectives the level of crime has risen. The rich have prospered while the circumstances of the worst-off have seen a serious deterioration. A substantial part of the Press is at gutter level, but that section has supported her and covered up for her. There is a mean-spiritedness and an 'I'm all right, Jack' ideology rampant in the country although there are signs that this is producing a revulsion against it.

Her 'vision' appeared to be of an idealised Victorian society where the wealthy are promoted and cosseted so that the lord and lady of the manor and their lesser imitators will have enough over and to spare to enable them to take bowls of soup to the suitably grateful poor.

George Orwell's Collected Essays include a piece on the debasement of the English language by politicians, which deals mainly with the modern use of worn-out metaphors, pretentious diction and the use of language to conceal thought. I wonder what he would have made of the use (or rather the misuse) of the language in statements from Thatcher and members of her governments. To put it plainly, a good deal of it has been humbug and gross misrepresentation of facts.

The pattern for 'Thatcherspeak' was set the day Mrs. T. entered Downing Street when she recited the prayer of St. Francis of Assisi: 'Where there is despair, let me sow hope', which was ludicrously inappropriate in the light of her subsequent policies and philosophy.

She climbed onto the 'green' bandwagon in September 1988, but the UK is still referred to as 'The dirty man of Europe'. Speeches on the greenhouse effect ran alongside her government's reduction of energy conservation and opposition to efforts to cut carbon dioxide in the atmosphere.

Another example of 'Thatcherspeak' was her assertion that power had been returned to the people. The abolition of metropolitan councils and the whittling away of the rights and standing of local government make nonsense of this claim. Her ex-Cabinet Minister, Francis Pym (now Lord Pym), shot it down saying: "A government that set out with a mission to decentralize and to roll back the frontiers of the state is, in many respects, doing the exact opposite."

Item: The Government announced a commitment to preventive medicine. A few weeks later charges were placed on dental and optical examinations.

Item: After the night of the 1987 Election results she promised: "On Monday, you know, we've got a big job to do in some of those inner cities." Innocents took this to be an indication of measures to relieve the appalling conditions in the big towns. Alas, nothing so generous. She merely intended action to bring them back to voting Tory.

Item: Encouragement for 'enterprise culture' and 'reform' of the system of education. The former diplomat, Paul Scott, Rector of Dundee University said on April 24, 1989: "Our intellectual institutions, on which our civilisation depends, have never before had to live in such a hostile climate. We are now faced with the most anti-intellectual, the most philistine government in our history."

Apart from crossing swords at Prime Minister's Questions and short conversations at Speaker's dinners, I cannot claim personal acquaintance with Mrs. Thatcher. I did see her for private talks on two occasions during the Falklands conflict. I recognize that she has tremendous fortitude, a prodigious appetite for work and a shrewd judgment of political attitudes. (This last, however, may be in question following the poll tax fiasco.)

Dennis Healey uttered a profound truth when he pointed out that "Thatcherism became possible only when the wartime generation was passing from the stage." For a nation that had taken part in the trials and standing together of that period, there would have been an immediate rejection of her chilling "there is no such thing as society." Mrs. Thatcher presided over the most odious administration in modern times. Having first come to public notice by snatching milk from schoolchildren, she maintained a record that was all of a piece with that.

The dire results of the years of Thatcherism are strewn across Britain like a hurricane. She left behind her a trail of devastation like Sherman's march from Atlanta to the sea. By 1991 the economy was shattered, education was in an appalling mess, and there were record numbers of bankruptcies and repossessions of houses due to mortgage default. Manufacturing industries were neglected, with training of personnel far behind our competitors, and we ended up with the two biggest recessions since the thirties. Unemployment figures were massaged to hide the real figures. The sale of council houses was an intelligent idea, had it not been followed by a freezing of moneys for the building of new homes.

She appeared to me as an inverted Midas whose touch turned everything to dross. But power as head of a government aligned with total lack of humour is a dangerous combination, and the country may well have breathed a heavy sigh of relief when she resigned in June 1991, and stalked off into the sunset.

Despite her talk of democracy and freedom she was the most authoritarian and dictatorial PM in modern times. She had the Stalinist practice of removing potential opponents. To say 'hmmm' to her dictate was permitted, but a whiff of opposition, or even of doubt, could carry revenge. Her attitude to Scotland was summed up in a nutshell when she grandly stated, "We love our Scottish friends!" with an 'every home should have one' condescension.

I cannot hide the fact that I looked on Thatcher's resignation as PM in the same way as the man who phoned asking to speak to the Israeli prime minister, Mr Begin. He was informed by a secretary that Mr. Begin had resigned. He rang off but phoned again a few minutes later on the same errand, and was again told that Mr. Begin had resigned. After another minute or so he phoned for a third time with the same request. The secretary, recognizing his voice, blew his top.

"This is the third time I've told you – Mr. Begin has resigned. Now stop pestering me!"

"I'm sorry," the caller said, "but I can't hear that news too often."

18: PERSONALITIES OF THE HOUSE

WILLIE WHITELAW

Over the greater part of my time in the Commons, Willie Whitelaw (now Lord Whitelaw) was the number two man in the Heath and Thatcher governments. A better anchor man would have been hard to find. He was the civilised 'front' behind which the Thatcher revolution was consolidated and without him it would have been even more unpleasant. It is worth noting the increase in banana skin incidents since his departure.

He adopts the posture of an innocent abroad but in fact is an extremely shrewd individual. He is not an ideological or any other kind of fanatic. Robust, decent common sense, fairness and willingness to arrive at a working consensus, made him a difficult target for Opposition snipers. It is said that 'he has the extravagant courtesy of the landed aristocrat' and his readiness to apologize ("I was wrong, I admit it") meant that when he had replied to an attack there was little more to be added.

A brisk interest in 'Whitelawisms' developed. These pronouncements left hearers bemused and one which received wide currency was the charge in a General Election speech that the Labour Party was "going round the country stirring up apathy." On television in the early 70s, refuting the accusation that the Tories had no economic policy, he replied: "We do have an economic policy. It has been expounded. It will be expounded. And I don't believe the Labour Party has one either."

In a similar vein, as Home Secretary, he told a Commons questioner, "It is quite untrue that we intend to make special constables into full-time police. Our policy is quite the contrary in fact."

His basic frankness was revealed in his "Mustn't gloat, of course, quite wrong to gloat, we all know that – but I can tell you something, I'm gloating like hell."

He hadn't an enemy in the House of Commons. I recall his being visibly moved by the tributes and good wishes from all sides on his appointment to Northern Ireland. All in all, a great House of Commons man and a safe pair of hands for any government he served.

DENIS HEALEY

If Members of Parliament had been asked to nominate a panel of the most outstanding and dominating figures of the House of Commons I have no doubt that the name of Denis Healey would appear at or near the top of most lists. This result would by no means signify a popularity contest as he had a substantial array of enemies – not all in the Tory Party – as well as friends. A man of his character could not have it otherwise.

First, there is his formidable intellect. His views are expressed with a certitude which implies that contrary opinions are lacking in a rational basis. It's true that on occasion with the benefit of hindsight, he will admit to having been wrong. His intellectual interests are wide and stretch far beyond the political arena and outside the arena his life would not be empty. A man, as they say, of many parts.

Then, he is a rough opponent; a bruiser going into battle with the delicacy of a tank. The beefy face of the Irish navvy type and the intimidating eyebrows enhance the effect. But he can take it too, and bears no malice. If you're not on the receiving end, his speeches are always a delight, a combination of logical argument and wit leavening the hammer blows.

I was present in the Chamber on the evening when a sample of the oratory mentioned above may have cost him the leadership of the Labour Party. It was the 10th of March, 1976, in a debate on the Labour Government's White Paper on Expenditure. In his wind-up speech as Chancellor of the Exchequer, Healey lashed the Tribune Group of the Labour Party who had announced their decision to abstain in the vote. One of the Group, the late Russell Kerr, almost apoplectic with rage, stalked out, muttering "bastard" and turning at the bar of the House to give Healey the two-fingered salute. When the vote was called, Healey paused on the way out to give a broadside to the Tribunites. From the account given to me his language was decidedly salty and unrestrained.

As 37 rebels abstained the Government was defeated in the vote but carried a vote of confidence the following day and so survived. Unfortunately for Denis, however, Harold Wilson, without warning resigned from the Premiership and the leadership of the Labour Party six days later. Healey threw his hat in the ring as expected in the light of his ability and the posts he had filled. From my own contacts I came to the conclusion that he would not make it to the top of the poll and said so to one of his foremost backers who demurred strongly.

"He will," he said. "Denis is the man the Party needs and wants."

When my friend took the same line after Jim Callaghan's resignation in 1980 I gave him the same message. Again he expressed his confidence in a Healey win. But when Michael Foot came out on top he excused his faulty forecast.

"Donald," he said, "I underestimated the number of nutters in the Labour Party."

Although the leadership of the Labour Party was never my concern, in one respect I greatly regretted Denis Healey's failure to win the job. I had imagined with gleeful anticipation the twice-weekly jousts between the Leader of the Opposition and the Prime Minister. If Mrs. Thatcher had had to endure these from Denis she would certainly not have had the same stomach for 'going on and on'.

ROY JENKINS

Forming a judgment from his political record, I would class Roy Jenkins (now Lord Jenkins of Hillhead) as a disastrous politician. As a Chancellor of the Exchequer his budgets were models of orthodox capitalist economics. But then, he boasted on one occasion that he had not used the word 'Socialist' for fifteen years, and according to Woodrow Wyatt, he was urging Gaitskell as far back as 1959 to dump Clause Four of the Labour Party constitution.

As Minister of Aviation, he saved the Concorde in spite of the astronomical costs which could never be recovered. If he wasn't the father he was certainly the midwife of the 'permissive society'. All along he has been a fanatic in support of British membership of the Common Market, and it could be said that it was the Referendum on the EEC which forced him out of the deputy leadership of the Labour Party.

His rather 'posh' accent with the inability to pronounce the letter 'r' has been the source of much innocent fun. There is a trace remaining, however, of the basic Welsh when he uses a word like 'situation' and delivers it as 'sit-oo-ation.' A story is told of a Commons tea-room discussion when a fellow Labour MP criticised Jenkins as lazy. "Not at all," said Aneurin Bevin, "a man who was raised in Abersychan and has an accent like that cannot be called lazy!"

He obviously has a capacity for inspiring loyalty as he has a coterie of devoted friends. With hindsight I now realize that in the Commons his friends were birds of a social-democratic feather. He has moral courage too, as he showed as Home Secretary in dealing with some gross miscarriages of justice, some of which had been neglected under previous administrations, and was not moved by threats of hunger strikes.

A stylish but nervous speaker (I could see his hands shaking when speaking in the Chamber) he would have been more at home in a more leisurely age than ours. After his return to the Commons as victor of the Glasgow, Hillhead by-election, he could be disconcerted as he rose to speak by cries of "Silence for Jock".

TONY BENN

It is a cliche that the days of great oratory have long since departed from Parliament. All the same, there are a few who can still draw Members from their pursuits elsewhere in the building into the Chamber, and Tony Benn is probably the star of them. A curious aspect of a Benn speech is his reluctance, in spite of his impeccable manners, to give way to Members wishing to intervene. It is as if the speech were a monologue which could not bear interruption.

His impact on the Parliamentary scene has been tremendous and a staggering achievement for one man, even allowing for his debating skills and intellectual power. In spite of his later denunciation of the Labour government he was a long-serving member of the Cabinet in that administration and stuck with it till the end. He was responsible, to mention a few items, for telephone districts in the directories being replaced by numbers, the introduction of postal codes, the Act which allows peers to disclaim their titles, the Labour Party re-selection of MPs and the Referendum on the Common Market.

I always anticipated a Benn speech with pleasure and I was never disappointed, even when at variance with the speaker's viewpoint. I have always enjoyed speakers who call a spade a spade, or even a bloody shovel, and Benn's brushing aside of cant and humbug was, in my view, exactly what was demanded.

With the present Labour leadership I cannot see Benn playing a part as a Cabinet minister in a Labour government. Yet it is people like Tony Benn and Eric Heffer to whom the party activists look and who provide the basis for the belief that the Labour Party will provide a Socialist government. It goes without saying that such an outcome, i.e. a Socialist Britain, is even less likely the next time round.

ENOCH POWELL

Without doubt the outstanding Parliamentarian of the 70s and 80s was Enoch Powell. Although most Members would not have gone all the way with the Labour M.P. who said that "he makes us all look like pigmies", his standing in the Commons was unique. Michael Foot thought he was by far the ablest man among the Tories. His background is well-known; his parents were teachers. He became a professor of Greek at 24 and, during war service, rose to the rank of Brigadier at 29.

He spoke, invariably without notes, in beautifully constructed sentences, his discourse running from point to point in a logical and even flow. He spent considerable periods in the Commons Chamber and, while appearing to be asleep, could spot instantly a non-sequitur, faulty grammar or an untenable argument, and equally quickly produce a witty comment.

Always courteous in debate, Powell usually gave way to a Member wishing to intervene. Of course, he had the self-assurance that he could furnish an adequate explanation of his argument or a rebuttal of a charge. On one occasion, James Prior, speaking at the Despatch Box, refused to give way to an intervention by Powell.

"I won't give way," he insisted.

"Why not?" shouted several Members.

"Because I know I'll get clobbered," was Prior's reply and it won the sympathy of the House.

His courage and integrity are beyond question. On occasions when the House was hostile to his views, he stood like a stag at bay. Like the Duke of Wellington, he had trained himself to speak the truth as he saw it, regardless of consequence. He expressed his views honestly in a climate where humbug and cant are common currency. This frankness can be disconcerting in minor as well as major affairs. After the announcement of the result of the election in South Down in 1987, a BBC reporter asked him how he accounted for his defeat. Powell's reply was true to form: "Because my opponent polled more votes than I."

Sitting directly in front of Enoch Powell in the Chamber of the Commons, I was well placed to be a Boswell to his Johnson. Speculation was rife following Selwyn Lloyd's announced intention to retire as Speaker. No doubt with his tongue well out in his cheek, Powell asked his colleague Jim Molyneux, "What about Dennis Skinner for Speaker?"

As any of us would have done, Jim expressed some amazement at the idea.

"Why not?" said Enoch. "He's a good attender, he knows procedure, and he's gratuitously offensive to every Party in the House."

One can sometimes guess from an individual's general attitude, what his or her opinion might be on any given subject. This does not work with Enoch Powell. Who could guess that he had long held that there was no threat of a Russian invasion of Europe or that he consistently votes against the return of capital punishment?

I had no hesitation in becoming a sponsor of his Bill to limit experimentation with human embryos. At meetings to discuss tactics he was diplomatic and ready to consider suggestions from the rest of us.

NEIL KINNOCK

Neil Kinnock entered the House of Commons in 1970, the same time as I did. Our acquaintance was slight until we were both members of a Parliamentary delegation to Norway in the early 70s, when I got to know him better. He is an amusing, likeable, decent man whose frank and witty conversation shows an irrepressible sense of fun.

Unfortunately, on his feet in the House he often becomes a victim of his own verbosity, so giving credence to the 'Welsh windbag' tag.

This loquacity did him and his party a serious disservice in the debate which arose out of the Westland helicopter affair. On the day of the debate, Mrs. Thatcher had confided to a close colleague that her Premiership might be over after the vote. John Smith's attack earlier had Mrs. Thatcher groggy on the ropes and it offered Kinnock the chance to deliver the knockout blow. To the amazement and the dismay of his own party and others, in a bombastic, blundering and largely irrelevant speech he handed her the reviving sponge and she was able to beat the count. MPs and journalists alike agreed that had he confined himself to pressing three or four questions which required an answer, he could have brought her down. It was all the more frustrating as the whole episode of Westland had thrown a poor light on Thatcher's veracity.

In the debates on the Scottish and Welsh Bills, Kinnock was an implacable opponent of Devolution. He played a prominent part in the scuttling of the Callaghan Government's Scotland Bill. Reacting to the increasing demand in Scotland for self-government, the Labour Party backed the Scottish Convention, but one may question Kinnock's fidelity to the concept when one recalls his reply to a question from the BBC's Kirsty Wark on his failure to mention the subject of Devolution in a wide-ranging speech to his Scottish troops. He revealed how peripheral to his thinking the matter was by responding: "I didn't refer either, to the rainfall in the Himalayas."

There is no doubt, however, that his over-riding objective in politics was to attain the Premiership. On his election as leader of the Labour Party he laid down clearly the main priority. "Our purpose," he said, "is the government of Britain. Every interest – sectional, factional, regional and personal – is secondary to that major aim." This was fair enough, had it not been followed by step by step dismantling of Labour policies. And one might question the timing (let alone the abandonment of principle) of a leader who was firmly for banning nuclear weapons when the Soviet Union was ruled by Brezhnev and opted for retaining them in the Gorbachev era.

Like Harold Wilson, Kinnock climbed to power in the Labour Party on a left-wing image. He went further than Wilson in moving to the centre. But Socialists may have reservations about a Labour Party whose political posture is – as Clare Booth Luce said of Roosevelt – an index finger, wetted and held up in the air.

Kinnock for PM? My verdict would be the same as Attlee's on being asked why a particular minister was being sacked: "Not up to the job."

19: THE SCOTTISH OFFICE

Although I regard myself as on the Left politically, if I were obliged to choose between the Tory and Labour parties as to the occupant of the office of Secretary of State for Scotland, I would opt for a Tory. Leaving aside other considerations, I would make this judgment purely from the angle of constituency interests. Experience of both these parties at the Scottish Office showed clearly that a Tory Secretary of State is likely to be more sympathetic and helpful to a rural or island constituency than his Labour counterpart. In my time representing the Western Isles, the big developments in my area were initiated by Tory Secretaries. On the Labour side, only Harry Ewing (as Minister at the Scottish Office) helped me with a major project by giving the go-ahead for the hospital and Old Folks' Home in Barra.

I do not pretend to give a logical explanation for this situation. It may arise from Labour party resentment at their long-time failure to make significant in-roads, apart from the Western Isles, on the Highlands and Islands electorate. Or it may be that Labour, at ease with union-organized workers of the Central Belt, have little rapport with the crofter/fisherman individualism of the North. It could even be that the Tories have an affinity with country people, or that Tories are more independent of their civil servants (although in the case of Willie Ross, one cannot imagine him being anyone's puppet). Whatever the reason, that was how I found things in my time.

The first Secretary of State appointed to the Scottish Office by the new Heath Government in 1970 was Gordon Campbell (now Lord Campbell of Croy). Partially disabled from severe war wounds, he was an indifferent performer at the Despatch Box in the House, but in matters referred to him at St. Andrews House, he was invariably helpful. At the time of the re-organization of local government in Scotland – although opinion in the Western Isles was by no means unanimous in accepting the status of a new local authority and parting from Ross and Cromarty and Inverness-shire – he took the decision to make the break and to approve the formation of an Islands Council. This meant a momentous advance for the islands and, on a personal level, it meant I would be dealing with local government issues with an authority based in my home town, instead of dealing with two towns on the other side of Scotland.

Following the defeat of the Heath Government in 1974, Harold Wilson appointed Willie Ross to the Scottish Office. In the 60s and 70s he was the most dominating figure in the Scottish Labour contingent at Westminster. Willingly or otherwise, the Scottish Labour MPs were under his whip and few would challenge his interpretation of the Party 'line'. Although he was a Nat-basher who relished dishing it out to the SNP, I confess that I liked him and recognized his gritty integrity.

'The Scottish Narks Party' was one of his milder epithets for the SNP. He gave us no quarter nor did we pull our punches in attacking him, branding him as a Gauleiter of the English government, draining Scottish resources at the behest of his Party bosses. We may have done him less than justice on this score as the Crossman and Castle diaries contain a number of references to Willie fighting his corner for Scotland.

After years of angry denunciation of the policy of Scottish self-government, when the Labour Party alighted on Devolution as the recipe to dish the growing support for the Nationalist case, he converted smoothly enough, (as did Neil Kinnock later for the same purpose). His assertion "I have always been in favour of Devolution" raised eyebrows and derisive snorts in quarters wider than the SNP.

His winding-up speeches at the end of Commons debates in which he had been under attack were a combination of pugnacity and humour. I was fairly fortunate in his riposte to a reference I had made to armed forces in a free Scotland. His "Donald, whaur's yer cruisers?" had the laugh on me. But that was easier to bear than his description of a Tory's speech as having only three things wrong with it: "He read his speech. He didn't read it very well. It wasn't worth reading."

As befitted the Member for Kilmarnock, he was in great demand for 'Immortal Memory' speeches, and his extensive knowledge of Burns' poetry came in handy in attacking the late Tam Galbraith who had taken a line deviating from the then Tory policy. Willie described the confrontation awaiting Tam with Mrs. Thatcher, who had become Tory leader, in the lines from *Tam o' Shanter:*

> *But Maggie stood, right sair astonished*
> *Till, by the heel and hand admonished*
> *She ventured forward in the light;*
> *And wow! Tam saw an unco sight.*

107

To his credit, Willie Ross forced through, against fierce Tory opposition, the Bill to set up the Highlands and Islands Development Board. This has now been superseded by Highlands and Islands Enterprise whose efforts are not yet apparent. But the Board had an impressive record of regeneration of the Highlands and Islands area, leading to employment, enterprise and hope in a long-neglected part of the UK. It failed, however, to deal with the land question, a sore point with me. The resistance of the landlords to the Board gave rise to a story that they were terrified when the name of the first Chairman was announced; it was a man called Grieve. They thought this was Hugh MacDiarmid!

George Younger is a model of the 'officer and gentleman' class. This does not mean any kind of Colonel Blimp – he is fully in tune with the modern age. But his courteous and moderate manner, while maintaining his own viewpoint, made him popular across the party divide.

Level-headed and able, he listened attentively to the arguments both in the House of Commons and at the Scottish Office. In the Commons chamber he would nod approvingly at good points in an opponent's speech, but his reply in winding-up would show that his own stance remained unchanged.

In my dealings with him at the Scottish Office I found him competent, sympathetic to a good case, and helpful. After a successful career in politics, he has gone on to the office of Chairman of the Royal Bank. Had there been more Tories around of his stripe, the erosion of Conservative support in Scotland might have been contained.

From an early stage in his membership of the House of Commons it was evident that Malcolm Rifkind was a man of exceptional ability, destined for high office in government. The first indication of his quality was a wind-up speech in which, without a single note, he replied to a six-hour debate, making reference to the Members who had taken part, rebutting or commenting favourably on their speeches. To those of us who witnessed it, it was impressive and an indication of a standard to be maintained.

He had taken a pro-Devolution stand in the 70s, but having moved up the promotion ladder, he became as time passed a hard-line Unionist, stridently defending the status quo. Had he still been serving at the Scottish Office it would have been done with 'supportive waffle'. He was a handy man with the formula 'all possible assistance short of actual help'.

The appointment of Ian Lang to the Scottish Office took place after my departure from the House but I had seen in the Scottish Grand Committee and in the Chamber ample indication that he was a Tory apparatchik running on the prescribed rails. In the debates leading up to the General Election of 1992, he claimed as proof of Tory commitment to devolving power to Scotland that "We allowed the Scottish Grand Committee to meet in Edinburgh." The location – or even the existence – of the Grand Committee does not advance the interests of Scotland one iota, and a man who thinks such a claim is of substance is woefully ignorant of Scottish aspirations.

A clear proof of his Governor-generalship on behalf of his London bosses was forthcoming at the time of the 1991 by-election in Kincardine and Deeside. The Scottish Office, in accordance with Thatcherite policy, had under consideration the transfer of Forester Hill Hospital in Aberdeen to Trust status. This was opposed by local opinion and the five candidates, including the Tory candidate. Within a week of the election being won by the Liberal-Democrat, Lang approved the transfer! He is, in addition, a graduate of the Thatcher School of Dissembling. The proposal to replace student grants, or part of them, by loans, was presented by Lang as a bonus: "For the first time, students will have the opportunity to participate in the funding of their own courses."

The office of Secretary of State for Scotland, created in 1885, while improving administration of Government policies in Scotland, has been impotent in the cause of Scottish government. The occupants of the office – apart from mavericks like Tom Johnston – have always been content to have the strings pulled from London.

20: WHAT'S GREAT ABOUT BRITAIN?

One of the minor annoyances of the House of Commons is listening to Members extolling the virtues of Britain as a country where everything is superior to similar aspects of any other country. The catch phrase is "which is the finest in the world", as in: our police force . . . which is the finest in the world; our army . . . which is the finest in the world; or our British justice(!) . . . which is the finest in the world.

It's a knee-jerk cliche. You can bet that not one in a hundred making these claims has ever made a comparative study of the organizations to which they refer. "British is best" and no questions asked.

The facts belie this smug self-satisfaction. Britain safer, cleaner, kinder, freer, more democratic, 'Mother of Parliaments'? It's mostly eyewash. Britain spends less in overseas aid than Holland, Sweden, Germany or Italy. Britain spends less on health than most European democracies. Long after it was banned in the United States, thalidomide was on sale in the UK, with the resulting tragedy. Crop pesticides banned in the USA are still in use in Britain. The system of having housing units manufactured in factories which led to the collapse of the Ronan Point tower block, is restricted to a maximum of 5/6 stories on the Continent. In the UK it was used for much higher buildings. The percentage of young people staying in school after the age of 17 is far below that of France, Germany, USA or Japan.

Following the King's Cross fire disaster, it became known that fire protection is far more stringent in the Paris Metro where, unlike London, regular fire exercises are held. At sea, safety improvements give way to commercial cost. Speaking on *Newsnight* after the *Herald of Free Enterprise* tragedy, Rear-Admiral John Kime (Chief US Marine Safety Organization) said: "The UK in general has not been a leader in the necessary international standard for ships."

According to Des Wilson, Chairman of the Campaign for Freedom of Information, the locations of some 2,000 major hazard sites are regarded as official information. Because of that, people living in these areas cannot be informed of potentially dangerous chemical hazards. This last is part of the British obsession with secrecy, making the UK a society where information which ought to be in the public domain without any danger to national security is withheld from people. Citizens are simply not trusted.

Take the case of the parents from Kent whose son died in the Falklands War. They were told that they had no right to know how their son died. When they applied to the courts the judge told them he had no power to force the Ministry of Defence to release the report. It seems British citizens have no more rights than serfs.

The lack of protection of individual rights has resulted in Britain being arraigned more frequently before the European Court than its EEC partners. Unlike the United States, Canada, Australia and New Zealand, Britain has no Freedom of Information Act. The frenzied whipping in the Commons against a Private Member's Bill for these liberties is an indication of the type of legislation which the Thatcher government had in mind in their proposed reform of the Official Secrets Act. Typically, the rhetoric with which the White Paper was launched and the real intentions of the Government are poles apart. One only needs to know the Tory government's record and philosophy to appreciate that the Bill would place severe restrictions on information and threaten the freedom of the Press.

As the *Scotsman* said of the White Paper, "despite its fine words, there is no mention anywhere in this document of a commitment to freedom of information, or the right of the British public to know matters which materially affect their interest."

"Wha's like us?" is a frequently derided Scottish claim. It can be heard every day in the House of Commons – translated, of course, into English.

21: The SNP and Devolution

[This chapter is a compilation of Donald's notes and material supplied by Chrissie, his widow, who acted as his secretary during his time in Parliament. It deals with the period 1974-79 when the SNP Parliamentary Group was at its strongest and when it played a significant part in the debate on devolution. -Ed.]

After the 1970 election, on the way to London to take up his seat, Donald, accompanied by his wife Chrissie, stopped off in Glasgow to consult with the Party Executive. She relates what happened:

"Because of an air transport strike we had booked sleepers on the night train to London and a large company of SNP supporters, complete with pipe band, came to the station to see us off. Spirits were high and in a mood of celebration they lifted us shoulder high and carried us to the train. Moments before the whistle sounded, Robert MacIntyre whispered to Donald, 'Don't say a word, but you are on the wrong train!' There was nothing we could do. The train with our sleepers had already left. Luckily we had first-class tickets, otherwise we might not even had seats.

We had spent the previous day travelling from Lewis by boat and train, and by the time we arrived in London in the early morning we felt utterly bedraggled and exhausted. However, we brightened up considerably when we were met at the station by Winnie Ewing and Jerry Fisher who took us off to breakfast.

In a way it was symbolic. Over the years we could always count on Winnie to be there with her support when it was most needed. She was indeed a faithful friend."

For the next four years Donald soldiered on as the sole SNP Member. Although he carried the burden alone in the House of Commons, he was later to joke about the advantages of being a one-man band:

"It was not as difficult as it might appear, and in fact it had distinct advantages. At any given moment I knew (a) where the Parliamentary Party was, and (b) how it intended to vote."

Apart from being joined briefly by Margot MacDonald after a by-election in November 1973, it was not until February 1974 that Donald received reinforcements in the House. It was a great encouragement and a tremendous boost to morale when that election sent six SNP Members to Parliament. The election of October 1974 gave four more seats to the SNP, bringing the total to 11. The Parliamentary Group, who became known as the SNP First Eleven, then elected Donald to be their leader.

No one worked harder for the Nationalist cause, as well as for his constituency, than GORDON WILSON who was elected in Dundee East. Apart from Donald himself, he was the longest-serving SNP Member, and over the years he and Donald became close friends. Donald used to envy Gordon's seemingly inexhaustible supply of energy and his prodigious perseverance in working on at a task until it was completed, no matter how long it took.

On one occasion, Gordon and Douglas Henderson, emerging from their office after an all-night session wrestling over some problem, were met by Hamish Watt, the SNP Member for Banffshire. Hamish observed their pale, tired faces with his farmer's eye and commented: "They look like they could do with a good feed of mash!"

When Dundee University conferred an honorary doctorate on Gordon, all who knew him agreed that it was well-deserved.

HAMISH WATT (Banffshire) was himself no stranger to hard work. He was often to be found mucking out the byre on his farm in the morning, and he would still be in the House of Commons at 5 p.m. He had formerly been a Tory, and had he not given his allegiance to the cause of Scottish Independence he would have made his mark in a Tory government. When he arrived in London to take his seat in the House, he first had breakfast with Donald and Chris at their flat, and afterwards Donald gave him a guided tour of the Houses of Parliament. Looking around the great hall of Westminster, Hamish's comment was: "My, what a grand place for storing hay!"

Another indefatigable worker was DOUGLAS HENDERSON (East Aberdeenshire), both as an MP and as a consultant. In his capacity as SNP spokesman on Employment he made notable speeches in the Commons and he took an active part in drafting amendments to the Scotland Bill.

He loved lively conversation, and he would often take Donald and Chris out to dinner where they would all enjoy an evening of stimulating discussion.

DOUGLAS CRAWFORD (Perth and East Perthshire) had been a frequent visitor at the flat even before he was elected to Parliament. He had a standing order for breakfast on his way to Brussels in exchange for a dinner on his way back. He was a good MP who worked hard for his constituency in what was a difficult Tory riding.

The best orator of the group was undoubtedly IAN McCORMACK (Argyll). Perhaps his training as a teacher helped him in this regard. His speeches were always worth listening to.

MARGARET (BAIN) EWING (East Dumbar-tonshire) was an able M.P. She and Donald worked well together. Her gifts as a speaker are well known.

GEORGE THOMPSON (Galloway), ex-teacher and gifted linguist, was a welcome addition to the group. The party, as well as his constituency, benefited from his many talents.

Without doubt the best P.R. man for the party was GEORGE REID (Clackmannan and East Stirlingshire). Television was his forte, and he enjoyed making speeches which were liberally scattered with quotable quotes.

ANDREW WELSH (South Angus) was a Member who worked quietly, not seeking the limelight, yet he was always there to fight for his corner.

WINNIE EWING (Moray and Nairn) astonished many people with her spectacular defeat of Gordon Campbell, the then Secretary of State for Scotland. She had blazed the trail for the SNP with her first win at Hamilton, and she made her presence felt at Westminster despite resentment at her politics. Also the fact that she was a woman without other parliamentary support made it difficult for her to pursue her goals in that male-dominated establishment. A woman of considerable intelligence and charm, she had a knack for getting things done, and her colleagues found her good to work with. Always straight and to the point, she would voice her disagreement without mincing words.

117

Sometimes the Leader of the party would come in for a sharp reprimand too, but they always remained good friends! She lost her seat in the 1979 election, but came fighting back to win as Member for the Highlands and Islands in the European Parliament. The Party recognized her tremendous efforts on its behalf by electing her as President of the Party after Donald.

Having become Leader of the Parliamentary Group, Donald found himself busier than ever. Apart from having overall responsibility for co-ordinating approaches and devolving issues, he was now in demand as a Party Leader at various functions, and he received many invitations for public appearances. But it was a shot in the arm to Donald that he now had ten colleagues whose victories represented the groundwork of the many faithful supporters in the branches throughout Scotland. He never forgot how much depended on the workers at the local level who gave so much time and effort to make the SNP a political force to be reckoned with.

From Donald's Notes . . .

The issue of Devolution pre-occupied Parliament for most of the Labour Government's tenure of office. A few days before the General Election of October 1974, the Labour Party had promised the people of Scotland that they would set up a Scottish Assembly which would be "a powerhouse with cash and authority." And Transport House added, "The Labour Party does not make promises it cannot keep." This last-minute conversion to Devolution was instrumental in winning a majority of the Scottish seats.

In November 1976, the government launched its White Paper on Devolution. The SNP Parliamentary Group immediately expressed its disgust with the inadequacy of the proposals. My comment at the time was: "For all that it reflects the new hopes and vibrancy of Scotland, the White Paper might have been written on another planet. Its only value is as a launching pad for genuine self-government."

The Devolution debate began December 16, 1976, when the Commons voted by a majority of 45 in favour of the principle of establishing elected assemblies in Scotland and Wales. Hopes were high that progress was at last being made, but these hopes faded as the Bill entered the Committee stage and the opposition it met there of petty wrangling over points was to set the pattern for failure. After twelve days and nights of debate the Commons got no further than page 2 of a 166-page Bill. The Government's Guillotine motion, introduced by Michael Foot, to limit the debate was defeated by 29 votes. 43 Labour MPs abstained; all Liberals, with the exception of two Welsh MPs, voted against, and with this the Bill's chances were destroyed. As far back as the previous June, George Reid had claimed that without the Guillotine the Devolution Bill would be "dead as a dodo", and so it proved.

The trouble with the Bill was that it was produced by people with no real commitment to Scottish government. For that reason it was blown about in the course of the debate by any wind that blew. At various stages it was announced that there would be no referendum; that it would be a mandatory referendum; that it would be a consultative referendum; that there would be no question on independence; and there were even hints later that there would be a question on independence. A hard core of 15 'antis' took up a great deal of debating time right from the introduction of the Bill. In his book on Devolution Tam Dalyell listed the opponents of the Bill. In the words of one reviewer they were "the most dismal collection of powerful mediocrities in Northern Europe." However, his opposition to the Bill was open and forthright, unlike some of his colleagues who, while making noises in favour, were busy planting landmines in the progress of the Bill. According to Patrick Cosgrave in *The Lives of Enoch Powell,* "Confidential exchanges took place between Thatcher's aides and a number of Labour back-benchers hostile to Devolution."

When one of my Parliamentary colleagues asked a Labour Member how he could vote against his own manifesto commitment he said simply that there were "promises and promises". There were enough Labour MPs of that persuasion to kill the Bill.

When the Bill reached its Third Reading the decision on voting on this stage posed a problem for the SNP group. Discussion showed some members in favour of voting against the Bill. It was a position that could be argued for, since the Bill was now even sorrier in appearance than at first showing. Reasonable amendments, drafted by Gordon Wilson, George Reid and Douglas Crawford together with SNP legal experts, and put down by the SNP to strengthen it, were defeated, while numerous amendments aimed at drawing its teeth (such as they were) and actively sabotaging it, were carried by the House. In the event, we decided to support the Bill, as, despite its anaemia, it was a start on a first degree of decision-making returning to Scotland.

As for the Liberal party's support, David Steel had an article in the *Times* in November 1975 headed "Why Scotland will brook no delay on Devolution". Yet he was to lead 12 of his party into the same lobby as the Tories and Labour 'antis'.

With the decision to hold a referendum the Scotland Act took a further step into oblivion. George Cunningham's amendment that 40% of the Scottish electorate must approve of Devolution was carried with the support of 27% of the House. 34 Labour MPs voted with the Tories in support of this undemocratic political chicanery. The 40% requirement should be kept in mind alongside voting results in the Committee stage of the Bill. The vote to give taxation powers to the Assembly was defeated although 40% of Scottish MPs voted in favour. The vote to consolidate the 40% amendment on the Bill was carried through although 47% of the Scottish MPs voted against it. Mr. Canavan's amendment to remove the 40% hurdle was lost although 63% of the Scottish MPs voted for it.

So although the Scotland Act was passed by both Houses of Parliament and adopted by Scottish voters by a slim majority in the Referendum of March 1, 1979, it was repealed (unconstitutionally) by the House of Commons after the General Election of May, 1979, even though Scottish MPs had voted for its implementation by a majority of more than two-thirds.

Kenneth Baker, on *Newsnight* (19 April 1988) said: "We go for a simple majority. That's how we do things in this country." Margaret Thatcher herself was known to quote Sir Winston Churchill's words: "In this House of Commons a majority of one is enough." Apparently this rule did not apply to Scottish votes.

The referendum result was the catalyst in the demise of the Labour Government. If Labour MPs had been prepared to back their clear manifesto pledge and to honour the declared wish of the Scottish people, the Labour Government could have gone to the country in its own time. On Thursday, March 17, when the Government resorted to a procedural device, the SNP Parliamentary Group called their bluff and forced a division. The voting figures were 293 to 0. The Tories, realizing the impotence of the Government, seized their chance, and tabled a vote of no confidence. In the ensuing debate, Miss Joan Lester referred to "the recognizable aspirations of a minority of Scots," and when I pointed out that we had in fact secured a majority vote, she counselled, "The Right-Honourable Gentleman should not try to re-write history."

It was a historic day on several counts. A catering department strike sent members streaming from the Palace of Westminster in search of food and drink, raising the possibility that some would not make it back in time for the vote. In the event the Labour Government was defeated. Winding up the debate Michael Foot looked in my direction and gave the Roman salute: "Hail Caesar, we who are about to die salute you."

It was the first time a government had lost a confidence vote since 1924.

Perhaps the last word can be left to Neil Ascherson writing in the *Observer* 26th February, 1989:

> The Labour Government was murdered by its own troops. A decisive group of Labour MPs, mostly on the left, thought that stopping Scottish Devolution was more important than preserving what many pundits these days call the last all-Labour administration in British History.

22: EPILOGUE

Donald Stewart did not live to write a concluding chapter in which he would probably have summed up his years at Westminster in his own inimitably modest way. However, perhaps it is appropriate that such an assessment is left to others. In the many articles that appeared in the press following his death, friends and colleagues recorded their appreciation of the personal attributes and political convictions which enabled him to play a unique role both at Westminster and on the Scottish political scene.

Spontaneous judgments made in obituary notices are often superficial and short-lived, but in Donald's case there is a remarkable consensus among people from all shades of the political spectrum. There is no doubt, for instance, that as the MP for the Western Isles he worked hard for his constituency. Bill MacAlister stated in a 1987 editorial in the *Highland News:* "No other person at Westminster has travelled farther and longer on constituency business." Donald himself said, "I tried to work for people and help them as individuals – not everyone is political."

But his influence was not confined to the Western Isles. An obituary in the *Independent* (25 Aug. 1992) describes him as one of the great men of modern Scottish politics. It goes on to say:

> He was a Scottish stalwart, standing on a bank of principle for a self-governing Scotland, speaking forthrightly for his cause, yet always in a gentle tone of

voice, always in words of intellectual clarity and moderation. Such a combination made him formidable in debate and successful in winning his audience.

At Westminster Donald felt completely at home. "I went into the Commons," he said, "as a one-man band and found friendship in all parties." Charles Kennedy describes him as a most curious combination: the nationalist politician cum establishment parliamentarian (*Glasow Herald,* 24 Aug. 1992). On a personal level he made a profound impression. Gordon Wilson, former M.P. for Dundee East, tells how, when he and his other newly-elected colleagues arrived at Westminster in 1974, they were given a warm welcome, much to their surprise. The answer, he says, proved disarmingly simple. "During the four years he had spent as sole SNP Member, Donald and his wife, Chrissie, had built up a network of friends among English Labour and Conservative MPs that lasted even during the times later in the Parliament when political stresses occurred." (*Glasgow Herald* 24 Aug. 1992)

In the same vein, Sandy Matheson, Convener of the Western Isles Council, recorded:

> We felt a burgeoning pride when we saw the respect and affection with which the Stewarts were held in the Palace of Westminster, from the policeman at St. Stephen's Gate to the Speaker of the House. (Gillian Harris, *Glasgow Herald* 24 Aug. 1992)

According to Winnie Ewing, President of the SNP, "He was one of the most-loved political figures of his day. To the SNP Members in the Commons he was our father-figure, our counsellor, and someone who could uplift our spirits with a formidable force of wit."

But his kindliness extended beyond his own party. To Charles Kennedy he was "something of a friendly parliamentary uncle" *(Glasgow Herald*, 24 Aug., 1992), while Calum MacDonald, who succeeded him as Member for the Western Isles, said that he often had cause to value his wisdom and advice (*Stornoway Gazette,* 29 Aug. 1992). "He was the most popular member of the Commons – he rose above normal partisanship of party." (*Independent*, Aug 25. 1992)

Perhaps his easy acceptance at Westminster was due to the fact that although his political stance was revolutionary – the breakup of the United Kingdom, no less – he did not look, act or talk like a revolutionary. He always emphasised that the democratic process was the only possible avenue of change. His was a conservative nationalism and in his speeches on Devolution he chose a deliberately undramatic style (*The Times*, 24 Aug. 1992).

In his article in the *Glasgow Herald,* Charles Kennedy, discussing Donald's laid-back style, wonders "if perhaps the Nationalist point of view might not have been more sharply articulated by say, a George Reid . . . ." Yet he concludes that the Big Bang basis of the election campaign [of '92] under the leadership of Alex Salmond met with no more success.

Alex Salmond himself is quoted in the *Stornoway Gazette* (25 Aug. 1992):

> Donnie Stewart achieved the rare distinction of being universally respected by political friend and foe alike. He combined an acute political sense and resolution of purpose with an unfailing courtesy in the expression of his beliefs.

These sentiments were echoed by Labour Party Leader, John Smith, who said, "Donald Stewart was a man of courtesy, charm and commitment and was respected by people of all parties," and also by Western Isles Labour MP Calum Macdonald, "Donald Stewart will be remembered as a man of principle and integrity" *(Stornoway Gazette,* 29 Aug. 1992)

In the *Daily Telegraph* (24 Aug. 1992) he is described as "a sincere, conscientious and disarmingly witty politician who was held in high esteem both in the House and in his beloved Scotland."

Brian Wilson called him "a man of uncomplicated integrity" *(Glasgow Herald* 24 Aug. 1992).

These words, 'conviction' and 'integrity', recur again and again in the tributes that poured in at Donald's death. There was no dichotomy between the man and the politician, the private man and the public image. At the funeral in Stornoway Free Church, Rev. Murdo Alex Macleod said of Donald, "He refused to put political expediency before principle." To quote Charles Kennedy again, "He always seemed a man at peace with himself and his world. At centre he was a man of thoughtful tranquillity."

According to Dick Douglas (*Scots Independent* 7 Oct. 1992) "He had an air of calm assurance – not the assurance of arrogance, but that of having a strong and certain position, outlook and values."

Perhaps his career is best summed up in the words from *The Independent,* (25 Aug. 1992):

> In his public life he evinced modesty, honesty, trust-worthiness – qualities almost unique in a modern politician. He set his style on his party and his cause

which he advanced mightily, securing for it a permanent and respected place in Scottish politics.

Mary Stewart MacKinnon

INDEX